Thomas Austin

D1466652

AFTER DEATH

AFTER DEATH

A POPULAR STATEMENT OF THE MODERN CHRISTIAN VIEW OF LIFE BEYOND THE GRAVE

BY

LESLIE D. WEATHERHEAD, M.A.

AUTHOR OF
THE AFTER-WORLD OF THE POETS,
THE TRANSFORMING FRIENDSHIP,
PSYCHOLOGY IN SERVICE OF THE SOUL,
JESUS AND OURSELVES. &c.

WITH A QUESTIONARY FOR GROUP DISCUSSION

5/6

LONDON
THE EPWORTH PRESS
J. ALFRED SHARP

First Edition, 1923.
Second Edition, 1930.

Made and printed in Great Britain by
S. J. FRASER & CO., LTD., 84/86, Tabernacle Street, London, E.C 2.

TO MY MOTHER.

' If I should die, and leave you here awhile,
    Be not like others sore undone, who keep
    Long vigils by the silent dust, and weep.
For my sake, turn again to life, and smile,
    Nerving thy heart and trembling hand to do
    Something to comfort weaker hearts than thine.
    Complete these dear unfinished tasks of mine,
And I, perchance, may therein comfort you! '

(Verse found written on the fly-leaf of her Bible, after her death.)

Preface to the First Edition

be intellectually untenable, and, on the other, to be unattractive or even repellent. Traditional pictures of hell seem morally revolting; while the heaven of Sunday-school teaching or popular hymnology is a place which the plain man does not believe to exist, and which he would not want to go to if it did.'[1]

Much that has been written on eschatology must seem to the anxious seeker vague in the extreme, and most vague where most light is needed. Have we not been too much afraid to popularize what is our honest belief concerning the life after death? It will be said at once that any book which seeks to follow the adventures of the soul after death must be largely speculative. This is readily admitted. But in times of great bereavement all men will speculate. May it not be a small service to such men to seek to guide such speculation by the light we have, and our knowledge of ' the ways of God to men ' ?

As Mark Rutherford says, ' To suppress speculation would be a violence done to our nature as unnatural as if we were to prohibit ourselves from looking up to the blue depths between the stars at night; as if we were to determine that nature required correcting in this respect and that we ought to be so constructed as not to be able to see anything but the earth and what lies on it.'

It will be said also that such a book will go beyond the teaching of the New Testament. This also is admitted. But in the first place, as Dr. Griffith Jones has said,[2] ' there are many questions relating to the

[1] *Immortality.* Edited by Canon Streeter. p. 135. (Macmillan.)
[2] *Faith and Immortality.* E. Griffith Jones. p. 9. (Duckworth.)

9

Preface to the First Edition

Unseen World which were not so much as thought of when the New Testament was written, and which therefore find no place there.' And in the second place, it must be said that in very many ways we have gone beyond the explicit direction of the New Testament, though not, of course, beyond the teaching implicit in the revelation of Jesus Christ. Take the well-known example of slavery. It took the Christian Church nearly two thousand years to realize that slavery was contrary to the spirit of Christ. The Church of the New Testament everywhere recognizes it as a necessary social institution, but no one would claim to-day that slavery was anything but anti-Christian.

Surely it is permissible to bring all questions to the light we have now, and in that light to strive to see them. So with eschatology, we need to state old basal truths in new ways. The teaching current some years ago on this subject presupposes a God who to our view would be unworthy of worship, a God, indeed, who stoops to methods which no Christian of to-day would demean himself by using. The whole of our eschatology is wrong if it presupposes a God who is anything less than the Father whom Jesus revealed.

This book aims at discussing in a brief, popular and untechnical way, the subject of the life after death in the light of modern thought. Its weaknesses and omissions are only too obvious, but if to any seeking or bereaved heart it brings clearer light, and thus greater comfort, its purpose will be fully achieved. A questionary has been added for the use of discussion groups.

Preface to the First Edition

Works consulted and quoted have, as far as possible, been mentioned in footnotes throughout the book. If any have been overlooked, the omission is regretted. The author desires especially to thank Miss L. G. Lawson, M.A., the Rev. Arthur Triggs, the Rev. C. Kingsley Williams, M.A., and Mr. Basil Matthews, M.A., for their great kindness in reading the manuscript, and for many valuable and helpful criticisms. Various suggestions are the fruit of discussion with my friends the Rev. J. E. Neill, B.A., in Madras, and the Rev. R. Newton Flew, M.A., in Mesopotamia. Though great gratitude is due to these friends however, it must in all fairness be stated that it does not follow that they share all the opinions herein expressed, for which the author alone must be held responsible. Thanks are due also to Mr. Percy Raby, M.A., LL.B., for his help in preparing the book for the press, and not least to my wife, without whose help the work could never have been completed.

L.D.W.

Manchester.

Easter, 1923.

NOTE.

Special permission has been received for the quotations referred to below, for which the author desires to express his gratitude:

To Messrs. Sidgwick & Jackson for the quotation from Rupert Brooke, p. 26.

To Messrs. Hodder & Stoughton for the quotation from Prof. H. R. Mackintosh, p. 59 &c.

To Mr. Andrew Melrose for the quotation from Donald Hankey, p. 32.

To Mr. John Oxenham for the quotation from ‘ Bees in Amber,’ p. 33.

To Messrs. Macmillan & Co., Ltd., for the quotation from W. E. Henley, p. 34.

To Dr. Leckie and Messrs. T. & T. Clark for the quotation from ‘ The World to Come and Final Destiny,’ p. 58.

To Mr. Gilbert Thomas and Messrs. Geo. Allen & Unwin, Ltd., for ‘ Every Evening at Set of Sun.’

To Messrs. Longmans, Green & Co., Ltd., for quotation from Dean Inge, p. 124.

To Miss Lily Dougall and Messrs. Macmillan & Co., Ltd., for quotation on p. 127.

To Mrs. Ainsworth for quotations from Percy Ainsworth, p. 138.

To the Master and Fellows of Trinity Hall, Cambridge, and Messrs. Deighton, Bell & Co., for quotations from Latham’s ‘ The Risen Master.’

To Sir Oliver Lodge and Messrs. Methuen & Co., Ltd., for quotations from ‘ Raymond; or, Life and Death.’

To Messrs. John Murray & Co., Ltd., for the quotations from Browning.

PREFACE TO SECOND EDITION.

I AM glad to be able to send this little book out again in its new form. It will seem to many to suffer from an aggravating dogmatism where a reverent agnosticism is the truer attitude, and from an overweight of poetic quotations and from far too many footnotes. In allowing these to remain, I have felt that in a subject like this we are often in the realm of speculation where every *authority* who can be cited should be cited, and where the truest guides are the poets who are, in some sense, the seers of the modern age. The dogmatism is not meant as an effort to force one's views on others but, in a popular book like this, is almost necessary for the sake of brevity. Conclusions have to be stated without indicating all the factors on which the conclusions are based.

I desire to thank those who by word, letter, and review have helped me to send out this revised and largely re-written edition. I am especially grateful to my friend and secretary, Miss Margaret Webster, for much careful attention to detail.

L.D.W.

Leeds, 1930.

13

CONTENTS.

		Page
PREFACE TO FIRST EDITION		7
PREFACE TO SECOND EDITION		13

I   THE FACT OF THE LIFE AFTER DEATH ...
DEATH   19
Some ' Intimations of Immortality '—The witness
of Jesus to a life after death—The meaning of
' Death '—The insignificance of death—Mors
janua vitæ

II   THE PREPARATION FOR THE LIFE AFTER
DEATH   34
' Growing a soul '—Principles of Growth—Hin-
drances to Growth—Jesus' method of soul culture

III   THE NATURE OF THE LIFE AFTER DEATH ...   47
The Resurrection Body—The Relevance of the
Resurrection of Jesus—Recognition and Re-
union—Growth and Progress—Will Growth and
Progress interfere with Recognition ?

IV   THE CONDITION OF THE LIFE AFTER DEATH   66
Hell: What it is not and what it is—Heaven:
What it is not and what it is—The meaning of
Forgiveness in relation to the life after death

V   THE CONSUMMATION OF THE LIFE AFTER
DEATH   91
The ' Second Coming '—The ultimate triumph of
Love—Heaven and Hell not the final conditions—
Will any one finally be lost ?—Final consumma-
tion and the preaching of to-day

Contents

Page

VI   OUR PRESENT RELATION TO THOSE WHO HAVE PASSED TO THE LIFE AFTER DEATH ... 108

Christianity and Spiritualism—Prayer for the dead—'The Communion of Saints'—Why the dead cannot speak to us

VII   THE PRESENT VALUE OF THE GOSPEL OF THE LIFE AFTER DEATH 134

Common attitudes to the life beyond—The sneer of other-worldliness—The true attitude—The life of the ages

APPENDICES.

I   THE RESURRECTION OF JESUS 147

II   NEW TESTAMENT TEACHING CONCERNING THE SECOND COMING 169

III   EXAMPLES OF GRAIN AND CHAFF IN SPIRITUALISM, ILLUSTRATED BY COMMUNICATIONS RECORDED IN SIR OLIVER LODGE'S 'RAYMOND' 177

QUESTIONARY 181

INDEX 190

                                'Tis time
New hopes should animate the world, new light
Should dawn from new revealings to a race
Weighed down so long, forgotten so long; thus shall
The heaven reserved for us at last receive
Creatures whom no unwonted splendours blind,
But ardent to confront the unclouded blaze
Whose beams not seldom blessed their pilgrimage,
Not seldom glorified their life below.

                              Browning (*Paracelsus*)

AFTER DEATH

CHAPTER I

The Fact of the Life After Death

I

THIRTEEN hundred years ago, a dramatic and picturesque scene was enacted at the Court of King Edwin of Northumbria. We can picture the old wattled hall ablaze with torches. A great log fire is burning in the middle. The atmosphere is tense with excitement, for the first Christian missionaries who ever visited England have just arrived from Rome, and are giving the substance of their message. At length there is a hush. The first discourse is over. There is an opportunity for questions to be asked. ' Can this new religion,' asks one, ' tell us anything of what happens after death? The soul of man is like a sparrow flying through this lighted hall. It enters at one door from the darkness outside, flits through the light and warmth, and passes out at the further end into the dark again. Can this new religion solve for us the mystery? What comes to men after death, in the dim unknown? '

After Death

Men have been asking that question ever since. To change the figure to that of Longfellow, we are

Ships that pass in the night, and speak each other in passing,
Only a signal shown and a distant voice in the darkness:
So, on the ocean of life we pass and speak one another,
Only a look and a voice, then darkness again, and a silence.[1]

It will be our purpose in the following pages to peer into that darkness; to catch what glimpse we may of the wonder of that life which stretches beyond the grave.

II

This chapter has been headed ' The Fact of the Life After Death ' but many will desire at once to have the evidence for believing that immortality is a fact. It is sometimes assumed that the resurrection of Jesus is sufficient evidence for this fact. The resurrection of Jesus is a fact which strengthens our hopes immeasurably; so much so, that if Jesus had not survived death, and manifested His survival, human hopes in immortality would have sustained a crippling blow. At the same time it is hardly sound to argue that because a unique being triumphed over death, therefore we shall do the same. The great, triumphant hymn,

Christ the Lord is risen to-day

makes one pause and think when the line is reached

Made like Him, like Him we rise.

If ever another is ' made like Him ' this may be true,

[1] Longfellow. *Theologian.*

Fact of Life After Death

but we do not leave behind us an empty tomb after occupying it for three days.

Another argument often used is that immortality is a universal desire of the human race and therefore must be true. But this too is dangerous logic. Universal desires on this side of the grave hardly argue the existence of that which is desired. Why should they on the other? Further, by immortality the Christian means conscious personal survival. Adherents of the great eastern religions who number millions do not desire such survival. They seek absorption into the infinite, which is far from being what the Christian means by immortality.

I think the ' proof ' of immortality is grounded in the character of God, and is bound up with it.

The nature of man is one angle of approach and we shall notice that in a moment, being content at present to realize that an argument based on the essential nature of man is an argument based on the character of God in whose purpose it has come to pass that man is possessed of moral values and therefore of survival values, since in this world his moral values are often not fully vindicated.

But when we put our argument from the character of God into the form of a dilemma it seems irresistible.

Some of us in the course of our work enter rather closely into the lives of others, and often come closest to them in their hours of sorrow. Here are two parents gazing with anguished eyes on the form of their little child lying white and still in his coffin. Into the hearts of both of them in that terrible hour,

After Death

comes one great consolation. It is that somehow, somewhere, somewhen, they shall clasp their little one to
their breast again. Can we suppose that behind the
shadows God is smiling at their fond delusion? If
so, He is not a God but a fiend.

An evasion from this position might be attempted
by suggesting that a child's death is not God's will
and that therefore He cannot be held responsible if
untimely death occurs. But if *ultimately* the purposes
of God can be defeated by a bullet or a germ or a
brick, then He is not a God fit to be on the throne of
the universe. His universe has run away with Him.
He cannot control it. We have saved His moral
character by calling Him an incapable fool.

'The blazing evidence of immortality,' said
Emerson, ' is our dissatisfaction with any other solution.' Martineau, it is true, has claimed ' to have no
objection to being extinguished,' but in this he speaks
for a very small minority. Most of us would say with
Victor Hugo, ' I feel immortality within myself.' It
may be dangerous to regard such feeling as evidence of
immortality. But the alternative is, to the Christian,
incredible. The very belief in the character of God
is implicated. All that we know of God tells us that
He could not drown that desire in annihilation, nor
mock a longing, which we feel was planted by His
own hand, with unending night.

> . . . . And he, shall he,
> Man, her last work, who seem'd so fair,
> . . . .
> Who trusted God was love indeed
>   And love Creation's final law—
>   Tho' Nature, red in tooth and claw
> With ravine, shriek'd against his creed—

Fact of Life After Death

Who loved, who suffer'd countless ills,
    Who battled for the True, the Just,
    Be blown about the desert dust,
Or seal'd within the iron hills?

No more? A monster then, a dream,
    A discord. Dragons of the prime,
    That tare each other in their slime,
Were mellow music match'd with him.[1]

. . . .

Thou wilt not leave us in the dust:
    Thou madest man, he knows not why,
    He thinks he was not made to die;
And Thou hast made him: Thou art just.

III

Human nature itself, as we have hinted, is an evidence of immortality. 'We believe,' says Dr. Trevor Davies in his recent book,[2] 'that man has arisen out of Nature and that he is raised above Nature by his moral and spiritual ideals. Is it reasonable, then, to imagine that the Universe has at last produced its supreme creation only to fling it away as some capricious child does a toy? If life, which has been so laboriously built up, so studiously prepared for, so long heralded, which is capable of such high tasks, which " rounded into a separate whole " can love, and pray, and trust, is destined to destruction—then is the whole rationality of Nature impeached.'

Our own personality is an evidence of immortality. We say, for instance, ' I think,' ' I do,' ' I say.' What do we mean by ' I '? We do not mean our

[1] Tennyson. *In Memoriam.* lvi.
[2] *Spiritual Voices in Modern Literature,* pp. 120 ff.

23

body. That is only a material thing of iron, phosphorus, carbon, silica, nitrogen, water, and the rest. That is not the essential self of man. We all admit the truth of Browning's line about

'. . . . the wonderful Dead who have passed through the body and gone.'

Nor do we mean our brain. The brain is but a part of the material body and no more thinks than a violin plays.[2] We use our brain to think as a violin player uses his violin to play. True it is to say that I cannot get into touch with the outside world without a brain any more than a violinist can produce violin music without a violin, but my brain is as useless without *me* as a violin apart from the human hand. Human personality must be behind both.

Further, concerning both body and brain, we have to remember that ' not a particle remains of the brain, or nerves, or tongue, or eyes, or hands, or feet, with which I did a good or evil deed twenty years ago, but it is impossible for me to doubt that it was "I" who did it, and that I to-day deserve the praise or blame which is due to it.'[3]

That self again has a clear sense of what is right and what is wrong; a sense which is derived from neither body nor brain. It is a self which demands another world in order that reparation may be finally made for all the injustices of this. It is a self, or

---

[1] *Abt Vogler, V.*

[2] cf. Browning. *La Saisiaz*
　　But the soul is not the body and the breath is not the flute,
　　Both together make the music : either marred and all is mute.

[3] J. Paterson Smyth. *Gospel of the Hereafter,* p. 12, in which the reader will find this idea much more fully worked out.

soul, if you will—for it can never be too frequently
emphasized that man *is* rather than *has* a soul—
implanted by the hand of God. The body is its outward covering. The brain is the instrument it uses,
but it itself is immaterial. And when body and brain
decay, when they are cast off as we cast off a
suit of worn-out clothes, there is no logical reason
why that soul should not go on in a further existence.
It is a solemn thought that we shall never be able to
get away from our soul. We may ignore it now by
heeding only the things of the body. We may stifle
it by teaching our brain to believe a lie. But through
all the ages ' I ' shall be ' I ' and ' you ' will be
' you.' Each will be that same self which now thinks,
and feels, and acts. Death cannot touch the self.
Dissolution cannot destroy it. We have embarked on a
journey concerning which it is difficult to foresee an
end.

As we study the characteristics of that human self,
we know that it is fitted for a far mightier life than
this. Just as within the egg-shell the bird in that
limited life develops an organism, even to the detail
of wings, which shall fit it for the fuller life when the
shell is broken, so as we look within ourselves we find
capacities, faculties, ideals, hopes, instincts, ideas of
goodness, high desires now unattainable or unused,
but have they no existence in ultimate reality? If not,
there seems grave irrationality in God's world. We
are driven to the belief that when the shell of this
little life is broken, when the limitations of this
' cabined and confined ' existence are done away, all

true hopes will be realized, and we shall rise with
eagle flight to know the fulness of the life beyond.
Then we shall

> Spend in pure converse our eternal day;
>   Think each in each, immediately wise;
> Learn all we lacked before; hear, know, and say
>   What this tumultuous body now denies;
> And feel, who have laid our groping hands away,
>   And see, no longer blinded by our eyes.[1]

IV

Another line of thought, even if it were taken
alone, would be sufficient to convince us of the life
after death : that is a consideration of the attitude
of Jesus.

Let us try to appreciate this. We might claim
of course that Jesus was divine; that He was a perfect revelation of the Father; that what He taught
was divinely revealed truth; that since He taught,
or perhaps more accurately took for granted, a further
life, the problem is settled. I believe this line of
argument to be both true and convincing.

But since the sceptic would have many stops in
his mind at the successive steps of this argument, it is
interesting to notice that without such august claims
the same cogency can be reached. Most sceptics would
admit that Jesus was the greatest teacher of religion
the world has ever known. Then let him consider
the authority of a great teacher on his own subject.
A man who seeks knowledge about relativity does not,
presumably, argue with Einstein. He sits at his feet.

[1] Rupert Brooke. 'Sonnet.'

Fact of Life After Death

I may quarrel with Sir Arthur Keith if he speaks dogmatically about immortality,—especially if he uses the illustration of a candle, suggesting that when the candle is done the flame goes out and when the body is done the soul is extinguished, as though such an illustration were an argument[1]—but when he is speaking on that sphere of science in which he is an expert I cannot but listen, for here he speaks not merely as any educated man but as an expert on his own subject.

Jesus must be listened to as an expert on His own subject, religion, and what does He say? It is more striking that He says so little. He is so *sure* of His subject that He does something even more convincing than the advancement of an argument. He takes it for granted as a truth as self-evident as the existence of God. All He tells us is that it is a falling asleep, a departure, and a going to the Father.

One feels that to say more would have been impossible and if possible unwise; unwise because it would make men dissatisfied with this world to learn of the glories that shall be revealed; and impossible as it would be impossible to explain what the colour red is to a man born blind. His lack of faculty would mean that to describe red as being like the blare of a trumpet would be as near as one could get. And how far that is from reality! So, with faculties developed for this world, how should we apprehend another? ' Eye hath not seen nor ear heard,

---

[1] It would be easy to find an illustration to ' prove ' the opposite, as for instance that of a violinist (soul) and his violin (body) through which he expresses himself. If the violin is smashed the player is untouched. Moreover, as Sir Oliver Lodge points out in *Phantom Walls*, p. 52, the light, for the production of which the candle was made, still exists somewhere in the universe even if we have no instruments sensitive enough to follow its path. The light is not destroyed when the candle is burnt out.

After Death

nor hath it entered into the heart of man the things which God hath prepared for them that love Him.' Jesus returned from the grave with one word on His lips—'Rejoice.' It is both a report from that undiscovered country and an assurance. And it is sufficient. If Jesus were wrong or deceived about an afterlife we cannot trust Him in those matters in which He is more qualified to speak than any other son of man. If the purest, noblest and most far-seeing is deluded, the delusion is an indictment of the character of God.

Some words ascribed to Jesus—remembering the accepted verdict of the scholars on the danger of ascribing language in the fourth Gospel, word for word to Jesus—we feel could never have been spoken by another. ' Let not your heart be troubled . . . In my Father's home are many places of rest. *If it were not so I would have told you.*' In that last sentence alone I find sufficient anchorage for my own faith.

V

The question now remains to be asked : in the light of this great fact of the life after death, what of death ? And the first thing to be said is this. Physical death is not, and was never meant to be a curse or a punishment for sin.[1] Death was a fact in the history of the animal creation long before man appeared on the scene, and man simply inherited a similar life-cycle to that of his ancestors. We must interpret

[1] ' Paul obviously connected physical death with the coming of moral evil into the world,' but it is ' a view difficult to the modern biologist, and not based as far as we know on anything in the teaching of Jesus.' Glover. *Jesus in the Experience of Men*, p. 43.

Fact of Life After Death

' death ' not as a physical fact, but as a spiritual fact; as the absence of that which, to the full-orbed life, alone makes it worth living; namely, communion with the Divine. Without such communion, indeed, the highest part of human personality cannot function, and is dead, having no correspondence with its purposed environment.[1]

Jesus used the words ' life ' and ' death ' in a similar way. ' I am the Resurrection and the Life : he that believeth on Me though he die yet shall he live : and whosoever liveth and believeth on Me shall never die.'[2] ' I am the Bread of Life. . . if any man eat of this Bread he shall live for ever.'[3]

VI

It is not difficult to realize that unending physical life would be by no means a blessing.[4] For one thing, room could not be found on this planet for the multiplied human life which would exist to-day. Some strange and terrible law which would make birth impossible would become a necessity, and the world would be a ' world without a child ' inhabited by beings in various stages of senile decay. If, to hinder this, some other law preserved man's faculties unendingly unimpaired, life, in such a youthless world would be an unescapable monotony, and death would be dreamed of as the highest good of all.

Death then is a beneficent and natural pheno-

[1] Cf. Drummond's conception of Eternal Life. *Nat. Law in Sp. World,* p. 55.

[2] John xi. 25.   [3] John vi. 35, 51.

[4] Cf. Tennyson's *Tithonus.*

menon. It is a mere incident in life. And concerning
it men commonly fear two things. They fear leaving
a known and loved world for what must always remain
something of an undiscovered country[1]; and, in rarer
cases, they fear some kind of immediate judgement or
punishment. ' The sting of death is sin.' It has been
truly said that ' but for the presence of evil in life,
men would think no more of dying after the day is
done than of going to sleep at night.'[2]

Gradually, as the Christian message spreads its
beneficent light throughout the world, as men grow
convinced of the *complete* pardon which is theirs in
Christ, as they realize that, being penitent, the curse
of past sin is entirely removed, death will take its
true place in their thoughts. The old ideas of death,
which clothe it in the dress of the bogey of the child-
hood of the race, which surround it with gloom, superstition, apprehension, and terror, should be relegated to
the limbo of forgotten absurdities.

' Death is the gateway of life,' and if we are to
believe the great body of scientific opinion, the actual
gateway is not so dark as we have hitherto supposed.
Sir H. Thompson says, ' I venture to state as a known
result of long and careful observation of the phenomena which occur at the close of life that a really
painful death from disease is rarely witnessed.' Sir
Frederick Treves in his ' Reminiscences ' says (p. 176),
' What is termed " the agony of death " concerns the
watcher by the bedside rather than the being who is

[1] Cf. Francis Bacon (Essay on Death). ' Men fear death as children
fear to go in the dark.'

[2] J. Napier Milne. *The Dream that comes True.* p. 41.

the subject of pity. A last illness may be long, wearisome, and painful, but the closing moments of it are, as a rule, free from suffering. There may appear to be a terrible struggle at the end, but of this struggle the subject is unconscious. It is the onlooker who bears the misery of it. To the subject there is merely a moment

> When something like a white wave of the sea
> Breaks o'er the brain and buries us in sleep.'

My own observations would support this. I have seen the faces of dying people light up with radiant joy. I have seen them sit up and stretch out their arms, I have heard them call the name of loved ones who had previously died; but I have *never* seen any one in any kind of distress at the moment of passing.

Tennyson well called this life ' the dull side of death,'[1] and we shall awaken into a life, which, compared with this, will be as sunlight is to shadow. Indeed, probably the greatest perplexity we shall have to face will be that of realizing that we are what men call ' dead,' and probably death makes as little difference to the purposes of God as would be caused by our removal from one city to another.

A further word may be said to those who fear death. If you had been able to contemplate arrival into this world you would have found the prospect fearful. ' It will be so strange, so utterly different,' you would have said. God knew all that. So, when you first became aware of anything you were lying with your head on a soft warm breast and all the nourishment you needed was three inches from you. There

[1] *Idylls of the King*, ' Lancelot and Elaine.'

After Death

were arms that held you very close. There were eyes
that looked down into yours in inexpressible love and
tenderness. You felt quite safe. There was nothing to
fear. That same Father knows that when you are
born into the next world you will be timid and lonely.
Will He not provide for you again? Will He not take
care of you? Of course He will! A mystic once said
that when a martyr was beheaded he was unable to
distinguish between the flash of the soldier's sword and
the sheen on Christ's garments. No one knows what
will happen. But Arms there will be to hold us very
close. And Eyes that will smile into our own.

The true estimate of death was seen by men of
high courage whose religion was none the less real
because it was to some extent inarticulate, of whom
Donald Hankey wrote,[1] ' They did not endure hard-
ship, they derided it. . . . Never was such a triumph
of spirit over matter. As for death, it was, in a way,
the greatest joke of all. In a way, for if another
fellow was hit, it was an occasion for tenderness and
grief. But if one of them were hit—O Death where
is thy sting? O Grave where is thy victory? Porten-
tuous, solemn Death, you looked a fool when you
tackled one of them! Life? They did not value life.
They had never been able to make much of a fist of
it. But if they lived amiss they died gloriously, with
a smile for the pain and the dread of it. . . . With
a gay heart they gave their greatest gift, and with
a smile to think that after all they had anything to
give which was of value. One by one death challenged
them. One by one they smiled in his grim visage and
refused to be dismayed. They had been lost; but they
had found the path that led them home; and when

[1] In *A Student in Arms*.

Fact of Life After Death

at last they laid their lives at the feet of the Good Shepherd, what could they do but smile?'

John Oxenham has finely put the following words into the mouth of one who lay upon his death-bed:

Shapeless and grim,
A Shadow dim,
O'er hung my ways
And darkened all my days.
And all who saw,
With bated breath,
Said, 'It is Death!'

And I, in weakness,
Slipping towards the night,
In sore affright
Looked up. And lo!—
No Spectre grim,
But just a dim,
Sweet face,
A sweet, high mother-face,
A face like Christ's own mother's face
Alight with tenderness
And grace.

'Thou art not Death,' I cried;—
For Life's supremest fantasy
Had never thus envisaged Death to me;—
'Thou are not Death, the End!'

In accents winning,
Came the answer,—' Friend,
There is no Death!
I am the Beginning,
Not the End!'[1]

* * * * *

'If it were not so I would have told you.'

[1] *Bees in Amber*, by John Oxenham.

C

CHAPTER II

The Preparation for the Life After Death

I

IT seems but reasonable to suppose that this life is a preparation for the next. If the *ego* continues its existence, if our essential self will be the same in the life beyond the grave, it is not too much to say that what we make of that self now, will determine its handicap and tendency in ' the undiscovered country.'

In this age we have got away from the old doctrine which taught that all man's destiny had been arranged for him, willy-nilly, by some inscrutable and immutable power. Rather than that once-called-Christian doctrine, most of us would prefer the definitely unChristian creed of Henley :

> Out of the night that covers me,
> Black as the pit from pole to pole,
> I thank whatever gods may be
> For my unconquerable soul.
>
> In the fell clutch of circumstance
> I have not winced nor cried aloud.
> Under the bludgeonings of chance
> My head is bloody, but unbow'd.
>
> Beyond this place of wrath and tears
> Looms but the horror of the shade,
> And yet the menace of the years
> Finds and shall find me unafraid.
>
> It matters not how strait the gate,
> How charged with punishments the scroll,
> I am the master of my fate :
> I am the captain of my soul.

Preparation for Life After Death

It is no meaningless platitude which says ' Sow an act, reap a habit, sow a habit, reap a character, sow a character, reap a destiny.' We are largely the controllers of that process. We are the captains of our souls. Their growth and development have been placed in our hands by God.

II

How does the growth of the soul in this life affect us in the next? In a sentence, is not the answer this? As we nourish and develop our spiritual nature by feeding it with spiritual food—giving things spiritual their due place—we increase our capacity for God; and on that capacity for enjoying God depends alone, absolutely, utterly, our happiness in the life after death.

A few illustrations may serve to make this point clear. Take the parallel of physical life. It is just as natural and necessary for a man to have God for the sustenance and growth of his spiritual nature as it is for him to have food and drink for the sustenance and growth of his physical nature. Moreover, just as a man by refusing food and drink would starve, injure, and reduce his physical nature (and his means of enjoying that part of life which is enjoyed through the medium of his physical nature), so a man who leaves God and things spiritual out of his life is starving, injuring, and reducing his spiritual nature, and dwarfing his possibilities of responding to a spiritual environment here and hereafter.

Let us pursue the same analogy further. Supposing a man says, ' I will develop my bodily strength and capacity, I will go into training, take up drill, and courses of physical culture,' and yet supposing that during that time he takes no nourishment, then the desired strength will never be his. Rather will he gradually grow weaker. Similarly, many men make good resolutions and endeavour to bend their will to a higher life; and yet they fail. The hungry spirit is craving for God. And the language of need is the same, whether it be that of the Psalmist in the height of spiritual ecstasy, or that of the prodigal in the far country. ' My soul thirsteth for Thee.'[1] ' I perish here with hunger.'[2]

To strengthen and develop the body we must take food and drink, however many Sandow exercises we may do every morning before breakfast. The only way we may build up a soul, in addition to all we may do in the way of earnest endeavour in the direction of the will, is to feed on God. If the body is diseased, it is only for a little time, and then it is thrown on one side. The soul lives on. If we nourish it, it will grow. If we neglect it, it diminishes, becomes less and less able to exercise its function, and when the body behind which it has sheltered has been stripped off, it will face God and the world of the spiritual with small ability to enter into, much less enjoy, the delights of that life.

Take another illustration to which we shall have occasion to refer again later. Three men go to an organ recital. The first is a musician to his finger tips. No felicitous grouping of chords, phrases or harmonies is missed. He traces with delight every repetition of the theme through all the variations of an intricate

---

[1] Psalm lxiii 1.　　　　[2] Luke xv. 17.

Preparation for Life After Death

fugue, and delights in each new presentation of it. He has studied and revelled in music all his life, and now he is in his seventh heaven. The second man sits next to him. He has not the musical soul of the other, but he enjoys the recital, enjoys it to the utmost of his capacity, though he cannot experience the same amount of enjoyment as the first. The third man is ' bored stiff.' He came there, perhaps, because he was dragged, or because he considers it ' the thing ' to pretend to enjoy what ' the best people ' call ' classical music.' Secretly he longs for the end. He has no part at all in a musical feast. The three men, though they may be good friends and sit together, enjoy that recital in three different ways, *according to their capacity for music*, and this capacity depends largely on their previous culture. Elgar said that when he was composing he *received* the music. He would go out to the solitudes of Nature and listen. The world, he tells us, is full of music and each takes what he wants. The music is there for the hearing but what we hear depends on our capacity.

So men will pass into the next life to enjoy it according as they have developed or failed to develop their capacity for God and for things spiritual. The saint is lost in a transport of joy. The average Christian, we may suppose, is able to respond to the spirit-life sufficiently to find great happiness. But the man who has cared nothing for God has no capacity now with which to enjoy Him. And there is no satisfaction in any other direction. Two things alone remain : God and his wizened soul.

After Death

III

So, if we may anticipate a future chapter for a moment, heaven and hell are mainly the experience based on that capacity for God, or the lack of it. What is heaven to one soul may be hell to another who cannot enter into its delights. He is in the presence of the most wonderful music in the Universe, but he can scarcely hear, and what he can hear he cannot understand. He is in the presence of the greatest beauty imaginable, but he is nearly blind. Jesus spoke of ' a great gulf fixed,' and no words could more truly picture the reality. The men in the illustration we have just used were imagined sitting next to each other, but what a gulf there was between them! And it was ' *fixed*,' for by no easy ' tap-turning ' method could the third increase his musical capacity so as to enjoy as the first enjoyed. It must take great effort and long years of training, and then it is difficult to see when the original handicap might be expected to disappear.

In this connexion Sir Oliver Lodge has written as follows : ' The first thing we learn is the fact of continuity. There is no sudden break in the conditions of existence . . . no break at all in the continuous and conscious identity of genuine character and personality. Essential belongings such as memory, culture, education, habits, character, affection, for better or worse are retained. Terrestrial accretions such as worldly possessions, bodily pain and disability, these naturally drop away. Knowledge is not suddenly advanced—it would be unnatural if it were—

Preparation for Life After Death

but powers and faculties are enlarged, and the scope of our outlook on the universe may be widened and deepened if effort here has rendered the acquisition of such extra insight legitimate and possible. On the other hand, there are doubtless some whom the removal of temporary accretion and accident will leave in a feeble and impoverished condition; for the things are gone in which they trusted. *They will be left poor indeed.*[1]

Without striking a note quite so dogmatic, it must be admitted that the general trend of Sir Oliver's words are in accordance with modern thought concerning the relation of the self in this life with that same self in the life after death. When, in the familiar story of the rich man's dream of heaven, the angel pointed out the place prepared for him, he expressed surprise at the smallness of the dwelling. ' Ah,' said the angel, ' you did not give us enough material to build a better ! '

> The only heaven thou shalt behold,
> Is builded of thy thoughts and deeds.
> Hopes are its pearls and faith its gold,
> And love is all the light it needs.

IV

Having regard, then, to the importance of growing a soul since so much depends on it, it might be well to consider some hindrances to growth.

The growth of the soul is hindered through a lack of use. That law of the physical sphere which is called the law of atrophy works in the spiritual world also. It is common knowledge that if we do not use

[1] *The Survival of Man,* pp. 235-6.

some faculty which is given to us, it will be withdrawn. If a man binds his eyes for a lengthy period, he finds, on removing the bandage, that he cannot see. In his *Natural Law in the Spiritual World*,[1] Drummond tells of some minute crustacea which inhabit the lakes in the mammoth caves of Kentucky. The cave he refers to is one into which no ray of light ever comes, so that whatever creature inhabits those caves must live in absolute darkness. Yet he tells us that these animals appear to have eyes. But on examination those eyes are seen to be a mockery. ' Externally they are organs of vision—the front of the eye is perfect— behind there is nothing but a mass of ruins. The optic nerve is a shrunken, atrophied, insensate thread.' When these same creatures are found in ordinary water through which the sunlight passes, their eyes are perfectly formed and in use. But in that dark cave, where they have no need of eyes, the power to see is lost. So it is with our spiritual faculties. To the extent to which they are not used they become impaired.

V

A second hindrance to growth we may call the law of porosis or hardening. At the first touch of a certain sin, the soul stands aghast, shocked, horrified. Gradually the keen edge of conscience is dulled. The soul ceases to hate the sin. The conscience ceases to react against it. The hardening process has begun. A man's besetting sin, is, let us say, constant loss of temper. He resolves on self-improvement but fails.

[1] p. 31.

With Rip Van Winkle he says, ' I won't count this time.' Psychological research has shewn us that it is being counted against him for all that. Passion will, as it were, run more easily down the channel which is made deeper by every fall. ' Nerve cells and molecules count it against him.' He is weakening his power of resistance. More than that, he is blunting his conscience against the shocks of sin, and ' we have lost our best defence against sin, when we cease to be shocked by it.'[1]

So a man emerges from some day-dream perhaps, wherein, in some imaginative situation, he has sided with sin and played with it in the realm of the mind. If no sinful action follows, he congratulates himself that he has escaped scatheless. But in reality it is not so. His soul will never recoil from that sin which he has admitted to the kingdom of his mind as it might have done, had the thought of it never been entertained and welcomed. It will be long before he can turn with the loathing of a pure heart against that evil. The terrible process of what we have called porosis has set in. The estimate of evil is lowered. The sensitiveness of the conscience has gone. Already some future battle is all but lost. The seed of good will fall now into ground that is shallow, or stony, or choked with thorns.

VI

A third hindrance to growth is a false and easy optimism which prevents immediate and earnest effort.

[1] Newman. Cf. R. N. Flew. *The Forgiveness of Sins*, pp. 12ff.

After Death

It is astonishing how many men promise themselves that ' later on,' when old age is creeping on, or ' when they have time to think of such matters,' they will consider the demands of their spiritual nature. They will ' have their fling ' and then at the end, perhaps on their deathbed, they will hope to crawl into the Father's home. It is difficult to imagine a more despicable attitude than that. In the first place, it misunderstands the whole meaning of religion by regarding it as a kind of insurance,—perhaps a fire insurance,—as a means of escaping unpleasantness in the next world. Such a person does not realize that religion is a thing which altogether transfigures and makes beautiful and meaningful this life,—a cultivation of our highest powers by co-operation with God. But apart from all that, let such men beware. They put off the day of allegiance to God, and think to turn to God in the end. We are not concerned in this chapter as to whether God will receive them, but let them at any rate remember that all the time the two stultifying processes are going on. They risk the atrophy of the highest of all human functions, and the heart is becoming hardened to the wooing of the grace of God.

When the terrible ravages of those secret cankers are reckoned with, who can posit that even if wishful, men will be in any appreciable sense *able* to find any happiness in a world of spirits? If such souls attain in some ultimate existence the felicity enjoyed by the saints of God, it can only be by some age-long and painful process, and even then, can the terrible handicap of a totally mis-spent earthly life be completely overcome?

Preparation for Life After Death

An Australian writer tells of an awful night in Scotland : ' The snow was deep; the wind simply shrieked around the little hut in which a good old elder lay dying. His daughter brought the family Bible to his bedside. " Father " she said " will I read a chapter to ye? " But the elder was in sore pain and only moaned. She opened the Book. " Na, na, lassie," he said, " the storm's up noo; I theekit (thatched) ma hoose in the calm weather." ' That is the best preparation for the life after death.

VII

We turn now to the secret of growth. Perhaps it may not be out of place to devote a few paragraphs to this part of the subject. A great deal of the practical application of the gospel of the life after death lies here. Christian instruction, especially to the young, seems often extremely vague. ' Christ will help you,' the young convert is told. ' You will not be able to conquer by yourself but you must rely on Him.' It is true, but it is not very explicit. A man wants to feed his hungry soul. We say, ' Jesus said " I am the Bread of Life," what else do you want? ' We point out that the soul, in order to grow, must be fed on that living Bread. We point out that part of the meaning of the Sacrament of Holy Communion lies there. As bread and wine nourish the physical nature, so the spiritual body of Christ, the very essence of God, nourishes the spirit life of man. But the question the young seeker wants to have answered is this. ' All this being so, how, how, *how*, can I feed on Him? '

After Death

Let us try to answer the question briefly by looking for a moment at human relationships. Two men become close friends. One has a besetting weakness. The other in that respect at least is strong. The weaker desires to please his friend. Moreover, he sees something in his friend for which he himself longs with all the passion of his soul. He makes an effort to overcome his weakness. But some other far more powerful agency is at work than the effort. The friendship itself is the saving power. How often, indeed, we use the expression, ' he was his friend's salvation.' The words are true. The weaker becomes like the stronger. Psychology goes as far as to teach that the weaker nature actually feeds on the stronger. In people who live together the working of this principle is readily seen. They become alike.

We may learn the Christian way by applying the illustration. We may so enter into the companionship of Christ that our weak little nature actually feeds on ' the strong Son of God.' Living in the bond of a daily companionship, we may become like Jesus. That was the manner of the disciples' likeness to Him. Christ's method in moulding the men on whom so much depended was not to extract from each a confession of faith, a creed, a belief, an oath of allegiance. ' Follow Me.' That was the only demand. ' Enter into My companionship. Ye are my friends.' That was all, and that was enough. And those who watched the whole process from the outside had no difficulty in accounting for the change that had come to these men whom they knew; a change inexplicable almost to themselves. ' They have been with Jesus.' That was the secret of growth. And thus began a life which is eternal, the life of knowing God.

VIII

The illustrations we have used, and the very language employed, may seem to suggest that growth is necessarily long and gradual, or even mechanical. We believe that it usually is gradual. Many so called ' sudden conversions ' have been preceded by a long spiritual evolution, in some cases kept a secret by a heart naturally reticent, but in some cases subconscious or even unconscious.

At the same time, no unbiassed observer can shut his eyes to the fact that *apparently* positions of spiritual advance have been gained and held in a few seconds. A vision of the Cross for instance, which reveals the Love that will never let us go, the Love that still goes willingly to death for us, may captivate a heart so that the conquest of that Love seems instantaneous, and we speak of a work of grace being *begun*, and of a growth being *begun*. Yet if all the psychic history of the case could be fully known, we should probably see in that sudden surrender, the capitulation of the soul after a long, long siege of the tireless Spirit of God and the prayers of men.

IX

We may all enter His close friendship, and drink of the wells of salvation found in Him. Day by day the soul may grow by this companionship whereby we

After Death

become strong in His strength. To explore the meaning of that experience is to grow a soul. It means the richest possible life here. But it is also to lay up treasure in heaven. It is the building of the mansions of the soul now. It is the enlargement of the capacity for God now. And no price that is paid for the quickening and deepening of the life of the spirit can, in the perspective of eternity, be considered too dear.

'He that soweth to the flesh shall reap corruption.' He shall crawl out of the ruined and decayed shell of body and brain in which he has hidden so long, weak and decrepit, blinded and blinking in the sunlight of God. But he that soweth to the spirit shall be as a gorgeous butterfly[1] which all its chrysalis life has been preparing for the glad hour of escape, and which now, in glorious dress of scarlet and gold, soars up on young strong wing into the sunlight which is its native air. He has sown to the spirit, and he goes to reap and to claim the fulness of that fairer life.

> Build thee more stately mansions, O my soul.
> As the swift seasons roll!
> Leave thy low-vaulted past!
> Let each new temple, nobler than the last,
> Shut thee from heaven with a dome more vast,
> Till thou at length art free,
> Leaving thine outgrown shell by life's unresting sea.'

[1] The butterfly was to the Greeks the symbol of the soul. Cf. Coleridge's poem 'The Butterfly.'

[2] Oliver Wendell Holmes. *The Chambered Nautilus.*

CHAPTER III

The Nature of the Life After Death

I

WE will now endeavour to follow the adventures of the soul after it has passed through the portals of death. The first question that comes to our minds is that relating to what has been called the resurrection-body or the spiritual body. It is no wild speculation to believe that we shall be no mere disembodied spirits with no means of manifestation to other spirits, but that, just as this body serves as a medium of communication in a material world, so some means will be provided or evolved for self-manifestation and fellowship with others in a spiritual world.

The whole subject bristles with difficulties and we can scarcely hope to clear them all away. Some things, however, are clear. Any idea of an actual resurrection of the particles of matter which now go to form our physical bodies—what Mark Rutherford called ' the fable of the resurrection of the body '— must be relinquished, at any rate while the popular conceptions concerning the nature of matter remain.[1] If the word ' matter ' means what most of us understand it to mean, then a physical resurrection is unscriptural, unnecessary, and undesirable.

[1] A modern suggestion has been put forward that matter is purely a manifestation of energy.

After Death

Nowhere in the Bible is the doctrine of a physical resurrection taught.[1] The phrase ' the resurrection of the body ' must always be understood to mean the survival of the conscious personality after death. ' Thou foolish one,' says St. Paul, ' thou sowest not the body that shall be . . . it is sown a natural body, it is raised a spiritual body. The first man is of the earth, earthy : the second man is of heaven . . . flesh and blood cannot inherit the kingdom of God ; neither doth corruption inherit incorruption.'[2]   (1 Corinthians xv.)

' Any notion that these same atoms will be at some future date collected and united with the dissociated and immaterial portion, so as to constitute once more the complete man as he appeared here on earth, and who is thereafter to last for ever, is a superstition.'[3]

' The dust returns to the earth as it was and the spirit returns to God who gave it,'[4] and by decomposition, the matter of which our bodies are composed

[1] The much quoted text in Job (xix. 25, 26) only needs examination in order to enable us to realize that a direct denial of a physical resurrection is made. 'I know that my Vindicator liveth, and that hereafter he will stand up upon the dust. And after my skin hath been destroyed, *away from my flesh* I shall behold God, whom I shall behold (to be) on my side, and mine eyes shall see (to be) unestranged.' (Driver & Gray. *Int. Crit. Comm.*) Whether we should go to the book of Job for evidence of any value on this subject is doubtful.

[2] 'Paul nowhere believes or states belief in a physical resurrection. By the " body " there can be no doubt that he means the personality. When he wants to speak of the material body of flesh and blood, he speaks of " the flesh." . . . The phrase in the Athanasian Creed, " the resurrection of the flesh " would have horrified him. He neither expected it nor wished the flesh to rise again; he wished the body to be emancipated from its bonds.' N. Micklem in *A First Century Letter.*

[3] Sir Oliver Lodge. Lecture on the Immortality of the Soul, delivered in London at Hackney Theological College, October 29, 1907.

[4] Eccles xii. 7.

48

enters into the structure of other human bodies and into animal and vegetable life.

> And from his ashes may be made
> The violet of his native land.[1]

Apart from all this, we shall surely have no need of a physical means of manifestation in a spiritual world, and it will be a moment of glad escape when this prison house is left behind, and the soul enters the freedom of the spirit world.

II

We are now, of course, in the difficult realm of speculation as to the manner in which we come to possess a ' spiritual body.' Possibly a consideration of other evolutionary processes may be of value here. May it not be that far back in the dim twilight of the world God either created a spiritual nucleus,— or what is more likely, in some sense gave of His own being—from which man has developed? Is not the whole long story of evolution the romantic history of the way in which this nucleus gathered around itself a means of self-manifestation within its environment? For long, long ages only the lower side of man's nature could express itself, because the means of manifestation was crude. The spiritual nucleus was hampered by an, as yet, imperfectly developed body.[2] But at long last, through the uncountable years, the organism developed, until the spiritual nucleus became possessed of the most perfect vehicle of communication

[1] Tennyson. *In Memoriam.*

[2] Note the expression, ' God sleeps in the tree, dreams in the animal, wakes in the man.'

and expression possible while still bound to a physical nature, and thus man became.

Thus, during that long period which we call the evolution of man, we conceive that the ' soul ' within him was weaving, for its means of manifestation and self-expression in a material world, a physical body. Similarly, may it not be that while man lives his physical life, his soul is at work, on the principles already suggested, weaving for itself a spiritual body which shall be a means of manifestation and self-expression in a spiritual world. Both are the expression of the same *ego*, but one is adapted for this life and the other for the life after death. This is surely the drift of the argument of Paul in I Cor. xv. As soon as a man is born into the world there begins the process of the formation of a spiritual body. As soon as an acorn is an acorn there begins to be formed within it that which shall become a grander, nobler life, the life of the oak. And when the acorn falls to the ground, the husk and the shell fall away, rot and perish; but the new life spring forth.[1] And the spiritual body, though an expression of the same ego which is manifested in this life in a physical organism, may be as different from it as an oak tree, giving its shade to men and animals, is different from the acorn which a man may hold in the palm of his hand.

III

The difficulty to most minds, however, in a discussion of the spiritual body, and one which ought in

[1] The Lord let the house of a brute to the soul of a man.
And the man said, ' Am I your debtor?'
And the Lord said, ' Not yet; but make it as clean as you can,
And then I will let you a better! ' *Tennyson.*

all honesty to be faced, is that which arises from a consideration of the resurrection body of Christ. The subject is too lengthy and complicated to be dealt with at this point, though it is dealt with later in this book.[1] Whether we may look forward to possessing the same kind of ' resurrection-body '—as the rather clumsy phrase has it—as Jesus; whether ours may be some ethereal medium through which we can adequately manifest ourselves to other spirits in a spiritual existence, but incompletely to spirits still incarnate,—all this must be left in the realm of speculation, a realm in which we have little to guide us.

IV

RECOGNITION AND REUNION.

It is clear that the spiritual body which we have assumed will be our means of self-manifestation and inter-communion in the next life, will enable us fully to be rejoined, and completely to recognize those who have gone before us. Any conception of the nature of the life after death which omitted reunion and recognition, would make even the highest heaven lacking in attractiveness. Indeed, to many whose earth life has been made desolate by bereavement, the rapture of reunion is perhaps the greatest anticipation of all.

> O thou soul of my soul! I shall clasp thee again,
> And with God be the rest![2]

There cannot be many members of the human race who do not desire to meet again, in a life in

[1] See Appendix I.   [2] Browning. *Prospice.*

which parting shall be no more, one who is still supremely loved.

Many people fear, however, that reunion will be robbed of its joys because recognition will be difficult. They fear that the loved ones will so have progressed and developed that it will be almost impossible to know them again. But this is not even true here. After many years face and form may alter, but one word and the gulf is bridged. We are driven to believe in growth and progress after death, but that a soul, because of those two factors, should be rendered unrecognizable surely need not be more true of that life than of this. No soul can lose its individuality or its affections, and it is foreign to our deepest and truest instincts and cuts at the roots of future happiness to believe, that for any reason at all, recognition and some kind of reunion are impossible.

> Eternal form shall still divide
> The eternal soul from all beside
> And I shall know him when we meet.[1]

' To-day,' said Jesus, to the dying thief, ' thou shalt be with Me in the world of spirits.' And that one sentence is the death-knell of all ideas of a long, consciousless sleep without communion with God or fellow spirit; and Jesus, in the parable of Dives and Lazarus, takes it for granted that we shall be able to recognize one another.

The words of Jesus about marriage have been thought to weaken the gospel of reunion. ' In heaven

[1] Tennyson. *In Memoriam.*

they neither marry nor are given in marriage but are as the angels of God.' These words do not mean that a husband or wife will be no dearer than any other personality. They do mean that in the life after death no tie will be binding except ties of the spirit. No merely earth-born tie will have any binding power at all. In other words, ' marriages made in hell will not be remade in heaven.'[1] An uncongenial bond, perhaps largely physical on this side, and thus unhappy, will not hold two natures on the other side. There are marriages and bonds wherein love never lived, and no such bond can survive death. If the bond of love is broken in this world, it may be repaired on the other side. Love alone is stronger than death, and love will meet the loved one again in a companionship of spirit more close and intimate than any earthly relationship—a relationship that need never fear the pang of separation, and a bond that shall never be broken.

> Hereafter in that world where all are pure
> We two may meet before high God, and thou
> Wilt spring to me, and claim me thine, and know
> I am thine husband—[2]

V

GROWTH AND PROGRESS

Growth is the law of all life. It is inconceivable to believe that the life after death is a life without continuous growth and progress. The alternative is

[1] J. N. Milne. *The Dream That Comes True.* p. 163.
[2] Tennyson. *Idylls of the King.* Guinevere.

stagnation. More will be said later as to the possibilities of the attainment of mature spirit-growth for all, but

> Ere the victory be won,
> Ere the work of grace be done,

there must for all men be a considerable growth of spirit, if the ' stature of the fulness of Christ ' is even to be approached.

In a world purely spiritual, however mis-spent the earthly life may have been, spiritual things will surely be longed for, because they will be seen in their true proportions. There is nothing inherent in the act of dying to bring about this greater clarity, but the blinding of the spirit to spiritual values occasioned by the flesh, by false estimates of real values arrived at by love of wealth, rank, social position, culture, education, pride of race, and the like, will continue no longer. The spirit will perceive the desirability of spiritual things as it never could on earth. The only wealth that can obtain currency there will be the wealth that is spiritual. Spiritual values will not only be, but will be seen to be, supreme, for spiritual influences will be more potent there than here.

The hunger for the spiritual, which conditions in the life after death will arouse, must surely be granted as much satisfaction as is consistent with the soul's capacity for assimilation. To deny this in order to punish the man who has not taken advantage of his opportunities in this life is to deny the possibility of growth in the highest kind of life we know, whereas, as we have seen, if one fact is seen to be uni-

Nature of Life After Death

versally true, it is that wherever we have anything which we may dignify with the name 'life,' there is also the process of growth inseparable from it. That denial indeed has far reaching implications. It would mean that a soul which had never had any chance of arriving at a true estimate of spiritual values could never hope to grow in the knowledge and love of God after death. Death would be worse than the end of all things. Without growth, annihilation would be more welcome than eternal life.

Shall we not be most fair if we suggest that at death growth and progress have a new meaning for all, with new and better prospects of achievement. And such growth will surely be continued, with no sudden leap from the point reached at death. Men will not be made perfect at death, nor will they be hopelessly damned. All that we know of moral and spiritual progress suggests that death will make so little difference that the scarcely-interrupted task of growing a soul will be continued.

Longfellow's beautiful lines in *Resignation* bear both upon recognition, reunion, and growth and progress after death.

> She is not dead—the child of our affection,—
>   But gone into that school
> Where she no longer needs our poor protection,
>   And Christ Himself doth rule.
>
> Day after day we think what she is doing
>   In those bright realms of air;
> Year after year, her tender steps pursuing,
>   Behold her grown more fair.

55

After Death

Not as a child shall we again behold her;
　For when with raptures wild
In our embraces we again enfold her,
　She will not be a child,

But a fair maiden in her Father's mansion,
　Clothed with celestial grace;
And beautiful with all the soul's expansion
　Shall we behold her face.

VI

The question at once follows as to whether there will be any difficulties at all in the path of the growing spirit in the life after death. On this side we are accustomed to think that growth is often furthered by, sometimes dependent upon, the overcoming of difficulty. It is, of course, obvious that all the temptations which come to us from the flesh will disappear, though the possibility must be admitted that in the case, for instance, of the sensualist, there may have been the stamping of the sin of the flesh upon the very spirit, so that still impure desire may remain but without any means of self-gratification. It may be that the overcoming of impure thought, which seeks to re-think old situations in the earth-life, when sensual sin was indulged in, may be a battle in which to conquer will make for the growth and progress of the soul.

Since we cannot believe that there will ever be a time in the history of the soul when it will be deprived of free will, the *possibility* of a choice less than the best, must—in the face of all that has been said as to the clearer realization of spiritual values—

remain. In the initial experiences of the life after death, can we positively assert that there cannot be any temptation to discontent, jealousy, or pride? We believe it improbable in the light of the spiritual vision. We believe it will disappear entirely in the consummated life, where surely no tragedy can be admitted. But we can find no grounds for any assertion that death, in some strange and sudden way, makes it impossible for the human spirit to be tempted.

' One may add here that we do not offend against the doctrine of moral liberty by affirming that every soul will come to repentance, any more than we do by the contrary statement that some men will always continue to sin. Indeed, this latter belief rests on the conviction that evil will go on always increasing its hold upon the will and binding it with heavier and heavier chains, until the power of choosing good has been for ever lost. And it is difficult to see how those who maintain such a doctrine can plume themselves on being the champions of freedom. What they really contend for is not the power of the will to determine its own destiny, but the power of evil to make an end of liberty. Do we indeed infringe the prerogative of the spiritual creature by saying that it will conform at last to the nature of things, that experience of evil will teach it that good is best and that the patience of God will bring it to repentance? And do we exalt the attribute of freedom by affirming, that, spite of the utter unreason of sin, spite of its bitter fruit, spite of the Divine grace and the perseverance of Christ, sin will be able to establish a complete dominion over the soul and bind it to itself for ever?"[1]

VII

JUDGEMENT

The popular idea of judgement is usually that of a huge assize, when all humanity will be assembled at the end of the world, and Christ the Judge will go into every man's case, consider its merits, make all the necessary allowances for heredity, environment, opportunity and circumstance, and will then pass final and irrevocable sentence accordingly.

These ideas are not unnatural. They are mainly due to a deduction from the picture, in the twenty-fifth chapter of St. Matthew's Gospel, of the Judgement Day, with its division of humanity into two classes, the righteous and the unrighteous, the sheep and the goats. The former are sent to a state of bliss; the latter to a state of punishment.

The parable, valuable as its teaching undoubtedly is, seems to the writer to have suffered from a wrong interpretation, and thus to have been the basis of a certain amount of wrong thinking concerning the nature of judgement. We shall therefore consider it a little more closely.

Leckie, in his recent Kerr lectures already quoted, has shown very clearly that in the apocryphal book of Enoch an almost identical passage occurs. ' Surely it is evident,' he says, ' that both owe their form to a common imaginative tradition. . . . No

[1] Leckie. *The World to Come*, p. 311.

one could infer from these prophecies that our Lord
distinguished between different kinds of sinners. . . .
It does not prove that Jesus did not utter prophecies
of this kind, but only that we cannot be sure that we
possess them in the very terms He used.'[1]

Any argument then, which may be deduced from
the parable to prove a definite *form* which judgement
will take, is certainly weakened by the consideration
that Matthew incorporated it in his gospel from some
' imaginative tradition '[2]; that none of the other gospel
writers contain even an echo of it; and by the further
consideration that to human estimates of justice it
seems difficult to understand that so fine a line may
be drawn between men, that those just above the
line are worthy of bliss unending, and that those just
below are worthy of what Matthew called ' eternal
fire.'[3] And the final judgement must be one which
is reconcilable with human ideas of justice. We shall
always be human and there is no value in a judgement
passed upon us which our best sense of values con-
demns as unjust or absurd.

The whole meaning of the parable, then, to us,
is an attempt to define a principle of judgement rather

---

[1] Leckie. *Ib.*, p. 110. *cf.* Also Streeter, *Immortality*, p. 197, Dougall
& Emmet, *The Lord of Thought*, p. 170.

[2] ' It may be either that Jesus permitted Jewish conceptions . . .
to stand, or that additions in that sense were made to His actual
teaching by later hands.' Prof. H. R. Mackintosh. *Immortality and
the Future*, p. 59.

[3] ' Not only general conceptions but also definite symbols like " the
outer darkness," " the eternal fire " and so on were borrowed from
the Zoroastrian Scriptures. In the case of our Lord's teaching especially, we cannot attach theological importance to the terms in which
He is said to have declared the doom of the lost. . . . If the message
of Jesus has any light to cast on this problem, it must be found
elsewhere than in apocalyptic sayings which convey no idea that is
in the least complex or characteristic, or which distinguishes Him
from other teachers of His time.' Leckie. *Ib.*, pp. 104 and 114.

than its form or setting. The test which Christ imposes is never as to how much of grace has been received, but as to how much has overflowed in a ministry of loving service for others; not what men have, even of the grace of God, but what they give; not to cry, 'Lord, Lord,' but to do those things which the Lord commands. 'Inasmuch as ye do it unto one of the least of these My brethren ye do it unto Me.' To have the love which delights to pour out itself for others is to possess the Kingdom of Heaven here and hereafter, and to be Christ's servant. To be without that self-forgetting love, whatever else one has, is, or does, is to forfeit the claim to be Christ's man, or to belong to His Kingdom.

We cannot, of course, dogmatically affirm that there will be no definite 'Day of Reckoning'; but probably a truer view is that which conceives of the judgement which must come to every man the moment he passes into the life after death. Between these two ' it cannot be said that the New Testament makes any formal distinction; rather does it leave the whole conception in the vague and imaginative state which is proper to its apocalyptic origin.'[1] A great assize would be a repetition, and, to our mind, a totally unnecessary repetition, of the judgement passed upon the spirit the moment it enters the spirit world. The day of death will be the day of judgement.

What is the nature of this judgement? An illustration may help to make this clear. If we come into contact with any beautiful thing we either appreciate it or fail to do so. The moment we come into contact

[1] Leckie. *Ib.*, p. 82.

with it, in one sense the thing itself judges us, as to whether we are lovers of beauty in that particular form or not; and in another sense we judge ourselves, for we are forced to acquiesce in the judgement. The picture of an old master is put before a man's eyes. Immediately that picture itself judges him to be or not to be a lover of art in that particular form. And he judges himself also in the light of that picture for he is bound to acquiese in that judgement. He is bound to admit to himself that the picture does, or does not, appeal to him.

So when a soul passes into the next world, spiritual values shine out more clearly than ever, and are seen to be supreme. In this light the soul views its own spiritual state. It comes into a spiritual atmosphere where goodness is the *summum bonum*, and it is immediately judged by that atmosphere as to whether goodness is a thing supremely loved. Moreover, it passes judgement on itself, for it can realize as never before its own poverty of that which, in the world of spirits, is the only thing that counts for wealth at all. So a man is ' made manifest before the judgement seat of Christ.'[1] He is judged both by himself,[2] and, in a sense, by Christ; but he is not judged as a prisoner is judged by a magistrate. ' If any man hear my sayings and keep them not, I judge him not; for I came not to judge the world but to save the world. He that rejecteth me and receiveth

[1] 2 Cor. v. 10.

[2] Cf. Tennyson.

    He ever bears about
    A silent court of justice in his breast
    Himself the judge and jury, and himself
    The prisoner at the bar.

not my sayings, hath One that judgeth him : *the word that I spake, the same shall judge him in the last day.*[1] He is judged as the man in our illustration who was faced with the picture of the old master was judged. The spectacle of the Infinite Beauty is the judge. But that beauty is necessarily incarnate. God has given all judgement unto the Son,[2] since our very humanity demands that judgement can only be fairly effected by comparison with a human personality.

When a man looks into the eyes of Christ, and knows, by the life Christ lived on earth, what his own human life might be, then Christ judges him without needing to pass judgement upon him, for in the light of Christ's standards that soul passes judgement upon itself.

> The *shame of self* at thought of seeing Him,
> Shall be thy keenest, sharpest Purgatory.[3]

So it was in the case of Zacchæus. Jesus uttered no word of judgement. But in contact with Christ there was this double judgement we have tried to describe. Silently Christ, and all that Christ was, judged Zacchæus. And Zacchæus immediately began to judge himself in the light of Christ. And from that double judgement sprang the first growth of salvation.

A further thought, not entirely irrelevant perhaps, is that every day is a judgement day.[4] For

---

[1] John xii. 47-48.   [2] John v. 22.

[3] Newman. *Dream of Gerontius.*

[4] Note the decided advance from the legal aspect of judgement in Paul to the idea found in John that every day is a judgement day.

62

Nature of Life After Death

every day we come into contact with good and evil, and by our attitude to them are judged. In the hour of that dark deed, in the moment of that slander that blackened a good man's name, in the moment of that concession to the call of the ape and tiger within, we were judged not by men but by Christ. In the hour when we refused to laugh at the filthy jest, when we did the true and straight thing and lost in earthly wealth and opinion, when others mocked and jeered and we upheld the honour of the Name, we were judged of Christ. The Judge, as we have seen, is not apparent. Often He appears to be the Prisoner as of old. We read of the ' judgement seat of Pilate,' and the world has a way of putting things thus ; but the scene that was enacted in Pilate's judgement hall was the judgement of Pilate, not of Jesus. So it is to-day. In the hour when men reject Him they do not judge Him. He judges them.

> O Lord and Master of us all,
> Whate'er our name or sign,
> We own Thy sway, we hear Thy call,
> We test our lives by Thine.
>
> Thou judgest us: Thy purity
> Dost all our lusts condemn.'

That is happening every day, and the final judgement when we pass over will be the logical and reasonable result of these daily judgements.

Men fear the day of judgement because they think of a *Dies Irae*, of a stern and wrathful atmosphere, of all that has been forced by the false preaching of the past into that heathen term ' retribution,' of wailing

' Whittier. *Our Master.*

After Death

and gnashing of teeth. But the searching Eyes are full of tears, the Voice that calls is broken with sobs, the Heart that yearns is breaking for love of men. Christ is not so much concerned with what men suffer, as with what they lose. To see Him, to know what He is from everlasting to everlasting, to realize that we have been so blind, so utterly blind, as to grieve by sin and indifference the heart of the unceasing Lover of mankind, that will be the bitterness, the awfulness, the condemnation of judgement.

> Thy sweetness is the bitterness
> Thy grace the pang of sin.

Or as the late Mr. Studdert Kennedy makes one of his heroes say,

> There 'aint no throne, and there 'aint no books,
>   It's 'Im you've got to see,
>   It's 'Im, just 'Im as is the Judge
>   Of blokes like you and me.
>   And boys, I'd sooner frizzle up
> In the flames of a burning 'Ell
> Than stand and look into 'Is face
> And 'ear 'Is voice say—' Well? '

Let it not be thought that any new interpretation of judgement robs it of its challenge or of its awe. Both are immeasurably increased. We may have lost some of the stage scenery of old apocalyptic ideas, such as still may be found in the hymn ' Day of wrath ! O day of mourning ! ' We may have lost the principal figure on that stage—the angry God burning to have His revenge. But what have we found instead? A Heart of infinite love wounded unto death by human sin. A Heart that will weep over men as over Jerusalem, saying, ' If thou hadst known, even thou, in those earth-days, the things that belonged unto thy peace ! But they were hidden from thine eyes—those eyes that would not see—and now the vision itself is thine own condemnation.' And it may be left to the reader to decide as to which makes the greater appeal.

The challenge and appeal of the day of judgement remain the same : ' Seek ye the Lord while He may be found, call ye upon Him while He is near : let the wicked forsake his way, and the unrighteous man his thoughts : and let him return unto the Lord, and He will have mercy upon him; and to our God, for He will abundantly pardon.'

CHAPTER IV

The Condition of the Life After Death

I

IT has already been indicated that we should be on more reasonable lines, if, in thinking of hell and heaven we thought, not of two exclusively different states or places, but of one spiritual world, which is hell or heaven, according to the spiritual condition of the soul when it passes through the veil. And since it seems probable that there can scarcely be those who are so good as to deserve unbroken bliss, and those so bad as to deserve unending torment, there will be for all some experiences which might be called hell, and some experiences which might be called heaven. May it not be, then, that as pain and pleasure exist in this world, not as exclusive states but intermingling in the experience of almost every day, so in the next world the joy of heaven and the pain of hell may intermingle until the final consummation? Speaking of men still in this life, we say that they are ' in hell ' or ' in heaven ' meaning that the one experience outweighs the other. May not the same consideration hold in the immediate life after

Condition of Life After Death

death? We shall consider hell and heaven separately, however, for the sake of clearness.[1]

II

HELL

That sad obscure sequestered state,
Where God unmakes but to remake the soul
He else made first in vain; which must not be.[2]

(a) We shall first consider some of the negative aspects of the idea of hell.

(1) *Hell is not a torment of flame.* It ought not to be necessary in modern times to disabuse people's minds of those caricatures of hell which are a libel on the God revealed in the New Testament as the Father of Jesus Christ. The days are gone when we could hold the old-fashioned ideas of a hell with undying flames, in which souls were miraculously kept alive so that they might fully experience the tortures prepared for them—torture conceived as viewed by the righteous and adding to their bliss. Such ideas, if not dead, are rapidly dying. The writer remembers seeing cuttings from a pamphlet called ' A Night of Hell ' by a certain Roman Catholic writer. It describes a girl who in her earthly life had been inordinately fond of dress. In hell therefore she is condemned to wear clothing consisting of burning flame, and to wear it for ever. The description informed the

---

[1] The terms ' hell ' and ' heaven ' are retained, but we realize that we lay ourselves open to the criticism that by hell we mean what is generally thought of as Purgatory, and by heaven what is usually called an Intermediate State.

[2] Browning. *Ring and the Book.* x. 2129-2132.

After Death

reader that ' the blood was boiling in her veins, the brains were boiling in her skull, and the marrow in her bones.' Nor was such absurd, but, to simple minds, terrorising teaching confined to Roman Catholic teachers. We have read of a Scottish Divine, who, preaching to children, tore a slip of paper from his notes and holding it in the candle by his elbow, informed his hearers that so their fingers might burn in hell, if they did not keep them from mischief.

Such a view of hell was not exceptional in the older preaching about the life after death. Fortunately it is becoming rarer as men see that all such views concerning the dealings of a Father with His children, apart from being impossibly materialistic, are an unscriptural and vulgar superstition.

(2) *Hell is not an endless condition.* The idea of an endless punishment originated in a wrong interpretation of certain Scripture passages. Most earnest readers of the New Testament have been glad to notice that the word ' everlasting ' found in the Authorised Version has been changed in the Revised to a more correct form ' eternal.' The Greek word *aionios* (αἰώνιος) which we may translate æonian,[1] means lasting for an æon or an age. How long an æon is we may not say, but we do know that by the use of the word the writer does not mean unending, any more than in our language when we speak of the ice age and the stone age we mean an unending period,

[1] Cf. Tennyson.

> But I should turn mine eyes and hear
>   The warnings of the homeless sea,
> The sound of streams that swift or slow
>   Draw down æonian hills, and sow
> The dust of continents to be.

68

Condition of Life After Death

though at the same time we may not be able to state the exact number of years the term connotes.

A close study of the words used in the New Testament and in much of the apocalyptic literature which so coloured the Jewish outlook and that of the writers of the New Testament shows that there is really no word at all which carries with it the definite idea of a period having no end.[1]

Let us try to clear away at once, however, an objection which has probably leaped already to many minds. It will be recalled that the same word translated 'eternal' in the New Testament, is used not only of hell but also of heaven. Everything thus that we say concerning the temporary nature of hell may be said concerning heaven. We must anticipate a little in order to say that in our view this is admitted at once. We believe that heaven will pass away. Finally a new era will be ushered in. The consummation of the age will mean that both the condition we have called hell and that which we have called heaven will pass away, giving place to a new condition, when the perfect life begins.

Reverting to our immediate subject, it must be admitted that the day has gone when an argument for the temporary nature of either hell or heaven could be built up from the isolated words of Scripture. The

[1] In Jude vi., a word is used, aidios (ἀίδιος) which emphasizes the idea of everlastingness even more strongly, and it is translated 'everlasting' in the Revised Version. But it describes an event which is said to be 'until' some other event occurs. The context thus makes it clear that no idea of unending duration was meant by the writer by the use of the word. If this word is loosely used, *aionios* must have been used more loosely still, as far as the idea of everlastingness went. For a further discussion the reader is referred to an essay on 'The Bible and Hell,' by C. W. Emmet, in *Immortality*, edited by Canon Streeter.

After Death

only convincing argument is that derived from a consideration of the character of God. Indeed, one word *is* enough : the Word made flesh, who answered for us once and for all the question, ' What is God like ? '

The thought of unending torture is revolting and horrible. It denies any consummation, any complete victory, and any real bliss in a final issue for God and His Christ. If a child were rebellious and wicked for ten minutes and a father tormented and thrashed, tortured and starved her for the rest of her life, his action would be merciful compared with that of a God, who for the sins committed in one lifetime tormented a soul unendingly. Moreover, unending punishment involves a contradiction in terms for ' every penal code points forward to its own negation, as theoretically it exists only in order to produce a condition in which it will not be needed.'[1] There is no utility in torture if the victims are not to be benefited by it, and surely God is not to be thought of as delighting in a useless revenge over souls no longer able to avoid Him. A man would not be allowed to treat a dog, by the lowest code of morality, as Christian theology of olden days imagined that the Father treated His children. We refuse to believe a thing true concerning God which we should despise in a human being.[2] Moreover, the whole idea of such punishment suggests that God knows no better way

---

[1] Dougall and Emmett. *The Lord of Thought.* p. 16.

As Shelley pointed out in his *Essay on Christianity* (Prose Works, Vol 1, p. 271) : ' All the arguments which have been brought forward to justify retribution fail, when retribution is destined neither to operate as an example to other agents nor to the offender himself.'

[2] If ye then being evil . . . how much more shall your heavenly Father. . .' (Matt. vii. 11.)

Condition of Life After Death

of attaining His purposes and accomplishing His victory than a method which we ourselves would not stoop to use.

(3) *Hell is not purposeless torture.* It is not to be viewed as God ' having His own back ' on men who can no longer escape Him. It is to be viewed as remedial and purifying. If the old phraseology is to be kept, then the fire is one which burns out the dross in men's lives and fits them for that which comes after hell and after heaven : the consummation of the ages.[1]

Perhaps the parable of Dives and Lazarus[2] though it may not be pressed too literally to be a picture of hell, may yet be relevantly quoted in this connexion. Jesus in that vivid picture shows Dives undergoing this purification by the fires of remorse. The process has already begun. In the earth-life he is shown utterly selfish, caring for none save himself. But now he is anxious concerning his brothers' salvation.

It will be said that this is very near the conception of Purgatory held by the Roman Catholic Church. Indeed our modern conception of hell embodies all that is best in that dogma. But we omit every materialistic and superstitious element in the Romish theory.[3]

[1] For other foundation can no man lay than that which is laid, which is Jesus Christ. But if any man buildeth on the foundation gold, silver, costly stones, wood, hay, stubble; each man's work shall be made manifest; for the day shall declare it, because it is revealed in fire; and the fire itself shall prove each man's work of what sort it is. If any man's work shall abide which he built thereon, he shall receive a reward. If any man's work shall be burned he shall suffer loss : but he himself shall be saved; yet so as through fire (I Cor. iii. 11-15). Every one must be consecrated by the fire of self discipline (Mark ix. 49).

[2] Luke xvi. 19 ff. Note v. 28.

[3] e.g. Indulgences.

After Death

We deny that the soul's destiny is settled at death, or that men are sentenced either to a final heaven or a final hell, and we deny that punishment is penal.

(4) A last negative thought to emphasize is that hell is not pain inflicted from without. ' Where Thou art is Heaven,' and where Christ is not, that is, where His presence cannot be realized by the blinded soul, is hell.

> The mind cannot be changed by place or time
> The mind is its own place, and in itself,
> Can make a heaven of hell, a hell of heaven.[1]

or again, as Omar Khayyam tersely put it,

> Myself am heaven and hell.

(b) We turn now to consider the positive aspects of our idea of hell. If it be thought that anything which has been said on the negative side has weakened the conception of the awfulness of sin and its terrible consequences, the reader is asked to weigh well what is written on the positive side, although his imagination may not be assisted by the lurid pictures used for that purpose in the past.

The words used are interesting. That often translated hell in the Authorised Version is better translated hades in the Revised. ' Hades,' ' Sheol,' ' Abraham's Bosom,' and ' Under the Throne ' simply carry the meaning of the abode of spirits after death, without connoting either pleasure or pain. Gehenna, the Valley of Hinnom, was the valley outside Jerusalem where the rubbish was cast and kept burning; where the worm died not and the fire was not quenched, *as long as there was anything left to be destroyed.*

[1] Milton. *Paradise Lost.*

Condition of Life After Death

The English word ' hell ' means a ' covered place.'[1] No theory of hell, then, can be drawn from a consideration of the words used.

(1) *Hell means a sense of deprivation.* A soul finds itself in a purely spiritual world, and is unable to enter into its delights in any degree of fulness because of an incapacity which has come as a result of slackness in the earth life. ' Hell ' said Coleridge, ' is conscious madness.' To know, as a lunatic often knows at intervals, that one is barred from natural intercourse, and to be unable to enter into any degree of the fulness, meaning and delight of a spiritual existence, must indeed be a form of hell. ' It is difficult for us to believe that the flame that tormented Dives symbolizes anything but the desolation of the anti-social soul that finds itself beyond the reach and glamour of those earthly goods which have blinded it to the psychic deformity it has been contracting.'[2]

(2) The sting of hell to many will be *the experience of being found out to be what they really are.* There are many people who seem to have the power of deceiving their fellows during the whole of their lifetime. Many, indeed, probably end by deceiving themselves. To be revealed not only to themselves but to others, must indeed be an experience which will make up part of the awfulness of hell. It may be valuable however, in that being found out will surely lead to a new start being made with true self-knowledge which alone is the basis of character.

[1] Cf. a ' hellier '—a thatcher.

[2] Lily Dougall. *Concerning Prayer,* p. 486.

After Death

(3) The supreme suffering of hell we believe to be caused by *the fires of remorse*. Perhaps it is a word the meaning of which we hardly know in this life, but it must have for all a very poignant meaning in the life after death; and it will take many forms.

(a) The vision of sin. In this life we cannot possibly imagine what sin means to God. We look at the Cross and we catch a glimpse there, dim though it is, of that meaning. A consideration of the eternal Cross, a realization that the Cross which was raised outside Jerusalem is only a symbol of an endless Cross in the heart of God, and the translation into terms of history of an eternal fact, deepen our sense of the sinfulness of sin. If we, with our nature so insensitive to evil, could only know, let alone bear, the sin of even one village, our mind would give way, our heart would be broken. What it means to a perfectly holy and loving Being to bear the sin of the world no one may guess. We may never know. There may be little use, indeed, in knowing, but the personal issue will be made clear when our earth-bound eyes are opened.

The late Mr. Studdert Kennedy, in one of his books,[1] tells of a father who in fits of drunkenness used to beat his little son whom in sober moments he loved dearly. The little lad lay dying and the father, now sober, watched by the bed side. In his delirium the child lifted his tiny hands, and, shielding his face, cried out in an agony of fear, ' Don't let him hit me, Mother, don't let him hit me.' The father knew then what his drunkenness meant to the lad. When we sin,

[1] *Rough Talks of a Padre.*

Condition of Life After Death

we are drunk, blind drunk. We don't know what we are doing. In the sober light of the spirit world we shall know what our sin cost God. We shall see sin as the ' crucifying of the Son of God afresh,'[1] as the ' raised hand, the clenched fist, and the blow in the face of God.'[2]

(b) Remorse also will consist in the memory of sin. Jesus puts stern words into the mouth of Abraham in the parable of Dives and Lazarus. ' Son, remember.'[3] We shall remember our lost opportunities, our past slackness, carelessness, prayerlessness, wickedness, and the poignancy of that punishment of remembrance will not be an easy thing to bear.

Memory is not essentially of the brain but of the spirit. According to Bergson, memory *is* spirit. A fragment of scientific evidence showing the persistence of memory even in this life will help us to realize that when earthly hindrances are done away it is reasonable to suppose that memory will, to a large extent, remain. Our 'memories remain in our mind from the earliest times. . . There is no such thing as a real loss of memory resulting from brain lesion; a pathological change in the brain simply prevents the memories from actualizing themselves. Memories are unconscious; but if the motor mechanism of the brain is excited, they may come to the mind as conscious memory. If the mechanism is out of order then the memories cannot come to the surface. This does not mean that they are lost, but simply that they are in abeyance. They are there from the beginning of time.'[4]

[1] Heb. vi. 6.   [2] Joseph Parker.   [3] Luke xvi. 25.
[4] Prof. Wm. Brown. King's College Lectures on Immortality, p. 154. Note the bearing of this statement on the question of the possibility of Reincarnation.

After Death

The fact that memory is not dead within us is evidenced by the fact that a number of cases of shock caused during the recent War, involving apparent loss of memory, have been treated under hypnosis, with the result that patients have gone back to definite periods of their lives, such as birthdays, with an extraordinary accuracy of detail, and have even gone back to the first year of life and have described events, afterwards verified and found absolutely accurate. Repeated hypnotic treatment has resulted in this being done again and again, the same facts being brought up to the level of consciousness with the same ease and accuracy.

Facts like these mean that the memory of the past will be indeed part of the pain of those experiences which we are calling hell.

> And the ghosts of forgotten actions
> Came floating before my sight,
> And the things that I thought were dead things
> Were alive with a terrible might.
> And the vision of all my past life
> Was an awful thing to face
> Alone, alone with my conscience,
> In that strange and wondrous place.[1]

(c) The most terrible part of remorse, however, will be the vision of *the effects of sin*. Dives, in the parable referred to, knew that his brothers were continuing their profligate life. May we not still be in some sense spectators of the earth-life? We shall see, one imagines, the ramifications of our sin going out, and going on and on to curse the world; changing in form, perhaps, but continued in heredity and influence;

[1] Paterson Smyth. *Gospel of the Hereafter*, p. 132.

always a debit entry in the account of the goodness and therefore of the progress of the world. On earth we cannot see it. In that clear light we shall. An artist paints a lewd picture. Its influence may seem to him small, if he ever considers what its influence will be. The picture is copied and recopied, distributed, exhibited. One youth, for one minute, sees one copy, in one shop window, and only God knows where the evil influence will cease. The remorse of such an artist in a world where he can see all the results of that picture will be a terrible punishment.

Imagine a sensualist. He has indulged in his sin for the greater part of his life. Continuously he has gratified his base desires at the expense of the women he has ruined. At length he marries and settles down, but only for a short time. Death lays its hand upon him and he passes over to the other side. Can he forget? No! He remembers. More than that, he watches. He sees the women he has wronged, and whom he caused to fall for the first time, embark upon a life of shame, and he realizes that he is mainly the cause of that tragedy. He sees his wife, his pure wife, who trusted him and believed him pure, smitten with the most loathsome disease that can come to human flesh, and he knows that he is the cause. He sees his children predisposed to disease, and worse than that, predisposed morally to fall into the sin of their father, damned before they were born, by his evil life. He sees them grow up from youth to manhood, from girlhood to womanhood, fighting the evil tendency which is his accursed legacy to them. Some, perhaps, pull through, but others fall. That beautiful daughter of his, the darling of his heart, goes at length the way that he sent other women in his youth. At least disease claims her, she dies, and he meets her in the unseen world; meets her when her blasted life is over, and he knows, as she knows then, why that sin had such dominion over her.

We need not employ the old imagery of eternal fire. There can surely be no greater hell than the vision of our earth-sin, working out its accursed course and blighting the lives of others who follow; running through the veins of human society like the poison of a serpent's fang.

III

Heaven

(a) As in the case of hell, we consider first some of the negative aspects in the idea of heaven.

(1) Heaven is not an endless condition. We look for a final bliss which must be greater than, and far different from, any possible happiness attainable while the experience to many in the unseen life is largely hell, and while this earth, with its tale of woe and misery runs its course. Therefore we cannot conceive of a set of experiences, or a condition of the soul being entered into immediately after death, which can be called an endless condition.

(2) Heaven is not a state of pure bliss. A mother certainly cannot be said to be in a condition of perfect bliss even though her own soul may be prepared for it, if her wastrel son is still passing through the cleans-

ing fires, and even though she knows that they are cleansing.[1] ' The individual can never know the full joy of the kingdom,' says Dr. Herbert Gray, ' so long as there remains one soul outside it.'[2] However true that may be of this world, it is certainly true of the next.

Indeed, surely the pain of heaven must be intense, for the higher we have climbed the spiritual slopes in this world, the more shall we be able to share the life of God in the next. And the life of God is certainly one of pain. He bears all the sin, all the sorrow, all the pain of the world on His own heart. The heart of God is breaking with an anguish none can guess; breaking with a yearning love which is constantly out on the search for the rebellious hearts of men, and a search which we know well enough is constantly baffled and disappointed. There is no stern Deity seated on a throne in pomp and power and glory, uttering in a voice of thunder the eternal decrees, living in remote grandeur a life untouched by human sorrow and sin and need. We talk glibly enough sometimes of the choirs of angels, of the endless music, of the eternal song. But that music, as long as one sinner remains on earth, is set in a minor key. The moan of a great tragedy sobs through it all. In the home of Omnipotence is the meekness of a Lamb hourly slain by human sin. With what joy is the repentance of one sinner acclaimed,

---

[1] Cf. Tennyson *Rizpah*. ' Do you think that I care for *my* soul if my boy be gone to the fire?'

[2] Gray. *Christian Adventure*, p. 26. Cf. Romans ix. 2, 3.

with what grief the impenitence of thousands![1] Nor would we desire yet a heaven in which there was no pain.

> Shall souls redeemed by Me refuse
>   To share My sorrow in their turn?
> Or, sin-forgiven, My gift abuse
>   Of peace, with selfish unconcern?
> Has saintly ease no pitying care?
>   Its holy lips without a prayer?
> While sin remains, and souls in darkness dwell,
> Can heaven itself be heaven, and look unmoved on hell?
>
> Is it a dream? Is heaven so high
>   That pity cannot breathe its air?
> It's happy eyes forever dry,
>   Its holy lips without a prayer!
> My God! my God! if thither led
> By Thy free grace unmerited,
> No crown nor palm be mine, but let me keep
> A heart that still can feel, and eyes that still can weep.'

(3) Heaven is not the gaudy city, the place or state of the popular imagination. We have imbibed from babyhood literal interpretations of old hymns and apocalyptic imagery, involving white robes, palms of victory, gates of pearl, star-clustered crowns, shining streets of gold[3]; the singing of hymns and psalms, and endless service on the lines of modern worship. We need to be sincere in this as in all belief. People do not imagine themselves in heaven if the preacher unduly prolongs a service. Nor does the verse

[1] Cf. Heb. xi. 40. 'Apart from us they shall not be made perfect.'
' Whittier. *Divine Compassion.*

[3] These symbols of St. John are meaningful. They represent peace, victory, consolation, worship, and the like; but do we remember that?

Condition of Life After Death

Father of Jesus, Love's reward,
   What rapture will it be
Prostrate before Thy throne to lie,
   And ever gaze on Thee![1]

represent as yet most people's idea of a better world than this.

(b) We turn now to some of the positive aspects of Heaven.

(1) Heaven is the ability to enter more fully than was possible in this life into the delights of a spiritual world, and into closer communion with God. The limitations of the flesh have gone for ever. We have all experienced those thrills of spiritual ecstasy, all too brief and transient, which are not of the substance of frothy emotion but which move the very deeps of our being; thrills kindled by some impassioned speech or mighty harmony, by the lisped prayer of a little child, by the sound of children's voices singing an evening hymn; kindled in some of us by the colour in the heart of a flower, the twitter of the birds at dawn, snowclad peaks aglow with the fire of sunset, the sound of the sea at night. And sometimes that experience is so deep and full that one feels that flesh and blood could stand no more. The uplifted spirit chafes against the flesh as a newly imprisoned bird flutters against the bars of its cage. Heaven is freedom for that bird. The thrill—and how inadequate is the word!—is the atmosphere the spirit breathes. The soul revels in spiritual fulness. In the earth-life we are as men away from home, who are unable to find a perfect environment, perfect sympathy and

[1] Faber.

understanding, and all that makes home. Jesus called the experience we call death, ' going to His Father.' Heaven to Him was going home. So it will be for all God's sons. ' We shall come into this home not as strangers needing to learn the customs and the language but as exiles returning, with memories awakened at every step.'[1]

(2) And that communion with God means new perception of truth. It will be no small part of Heaven to those whose lives have been given to the search for truth and beauty to find there that quest carried on with greater facilities and ever increasing light on the baffling problems of a lifetime, and an ever growing wonder and appreciation of ' whatsoever things are lovely,' and ' whatsoever things are true.'

(3) Fellowship with man, too, will be a positive joy of heaven. We have explored very little of what such fellowship in the bonds of perfect love might mean. We shall realize it more fully there. And in that fellowship there will be room for the expression of all that is of God in our personality; humour and gaiety, as well as sympathy and pity will have their place.

(4) Heaven is also self-revelation. That revelation will be a bitter experience, indeed, to many, but a joyous experience to others. That lonely toiler in the dark, that man who pretended no religion and held no creed, but who lived the straight life and served God in the service of his fellows, who saw that to worship God is to serve God and to serve God is to serve humanity, what a surprise for him ! That lowly

[1] A. Clutton-Brock. *Immortality*, p. 230.

housewife who practised always the gospel of cheerfulness, what an unexpected reward for her! One thinks of men who would say to one, 'I'm not a religious bloke, Padre,' and yet lived a life, (not only in the trenches where definite calls for heroism and unselfishness are continually being made, but in the ordinary life of the camp) full of unselfish deeds, very dear to the heart and spirit of Christ, showing that fellowship of the kingdom which is the very first necessity of the Christian.

(5) The greatest conception of the joyous experiences which we have called heaven is that of service : full and free participation in the work of Christ. This may be done among other spirits, among other worlds perhaps; or we may be allowed in some way to help to save this. The glory of heaven to Christ's servants will not be that they cease from their labours and enter into bliss. What is understood by most people as pure bliss would be intolerable to an intelligent person for more than a fortnight. The glory of heaven will surely mean that with renewed strength and unwearied zeal they continue that dear service begun in His strength below, until the final consummation of the ages. Our desire will be in Tennyson's words,

> She desires no isles of the blest, no quiet seats of the just,
> To rest in a golden grove, or to bask in a summer sky;
> Give her the wages of going on, and not to die.[1]

IV

We have to stay for a moment to consider the bearing of the gospel of forgiveness on our conception

[1] *Wages.*

of the life after death. The language we have used as to the growing of a soul, and the building up of spiritual capacity; and the illustrations we have used (comparing spiritual with musical capacity, for instance) may mislead the reader into the conclusion that forgiveness or no forgiveness, a man in the next world reaps precisely what he sows in this.

The point is that forgiveness makes all the difference in our *relation* with God. It does not, we conceive, magically increase spiritual capacity, but it deepens that process, because, if it is real, it means a new spiritual vision. *But forgiveness is first and foremost, the restoration of a relationship.* The child is restored to his proper and conscious relation with his Father. And that restoration of a relationship is accomplished at that moment when, truly penitent, the child can really feel that his forgiveness is not too good to be true; when, in a word, he can accept it. The forgiveness of God is complete. It means the entire washing away of the guilt of the sin of the past, though not, as we shall see, of the effect of past sin. But to the forgiven sinner there is now no barrier between himself and God. Where once was discord is now harmony.

> The Moving Finger writes; and, having writ
> Moves on: nor all your Piety nor Wit
> Shall lure it back to cancel half a Line,
> Nor all your Tears wash out a Word of it.

So Omar Khayyam. ' The Unseen Opponent in the great game of life while scrupulously fair, will allow no back moves, and makes us pay in full for every blunder.' So Huxley. But God's relation to sin which has been truly repented for, is the glorious antithesis of this. ' He hath not dealt with us after our sins, nor rewarded us according to our iniquities. For as the heaven is high above the earth, so great is his mercy towards them that fear him. As far as the east is from the west, so far hath he removed our transgressions from us.' He hath put sin ' behind His back.' It is to be ' remembered no more against us.' It is ' blotted out.' The pardoned sinner is brought back to *a relationship* which is unimpaired by the past sin. The relationship is as though the son had never strayed from his Father's house. And the day will never come, in this world or the next, when the sin which has been pardoned is again brought to light, and hurled by God into the sinner's face.

Human conceptions of forgiveness make it well-nigh impossible for us to conceive what God's forgiveness really means. Even the mother finds it hard to treat the wilful child, even though penitent, as though he had never sinned at all. We say that we forgive, but the relationship which once existed is broken for ever. But God forgives completely. The child is treated as though he had never sinned. Not that God forgets, but a more wondrous thing still : remembering, He forgives. The relationship is unimpaired. ' God's forgiveness is never a mere passing of the word, a dumb turning of the back, a formal cancelling of a debt. It implies a personal relationship, violated but now restored. . . We see a forgiveness which is wider and freer than the sinner

After Death

dares to ask, so wide and generous that the narrow heart of man stumbles at it when he sees it bestowed on another. The Divine love is without limit and the Divine forgiveness is complete.'[1]

It is in regard to the consideration of the bearing of forgiveness on the life after death that some of our narrow hearts stumble. Men are apt, for instance, to think it ' unfair ' that a man who repents, however genuinely, at the very end of his life should be received back into the relationship of a son. Yet in our more generous moments it is what we ourselves would desire for him. And it is what God desires for, and accomplishes in, him. The thought that is often at the back of our minds when we think thus ungenerously, is that the sinner ' has had a good time,' or even ' has had the best of it ' in this life, and then repents in order to have the best in the other. But he cannot repent to order. Repentance becomes the harder as he proceeds in sin. His repentance must be indeed genuine to win him back the rights and privileges of a son. And *has* he had the best of this world? Has he had a good time? Does the worldling get more out of life than the Christian? He has an easier time, perhaps. But taking a true perspective of the whole of life it is not even easier. It is the way of the transgressor that is hard. It is kicking against the goad that is hard. And what of inward peace, what of the companionship of Christ, what of consolation in sorrow?

[1] R. N. Flew. *The Forgiveness of Sins*, pp. 5 ff. (The whole booklet should be read for a brief but complete statement of the meaning of God's forgiveness.)

Condition of Life After Death

' Ye that have known Him is He sweet to know ? '
Is not the whole world well lost if He be gained ?

Then do the days spent in sin mean no loss at
all, so long as repentance is real before death ?

In trying to answer that question we shall be
on the right lines if we try to arrive at our conclusions
from a consideration of conditions in the human family.
It was to the human family that Jesus constantly went
to show men what God was like, and any conception
of God is false unless it can be harmonized with Jesus'
picture of God's Fatherhood.

We shall imagine a Christian father whose son
goes astray, but who at last, injured in body and mind
as well as in soul, by sin, repents, and comes back
to his father's house. What happens ? He is received
at once with open arms. The *relationship* is entirely
restored at once. The father treats the son as though
he had never strayed.

But other factors inevitably come in. At first the
son can scarcely believe in his father's goodness. It
is with difficulty that he can accept the pardon offered
him. And this is very true of God. It is no light
thing to accept such pardon; it is no easy thing.

> In wonder lost, with trembling joy
> We take the pardon of our God.

And it is difficult for this reason. Although God
accepts His son at once into a full relationship which
carries with it a desire for full communion, the son
cannot enter fully *at once* into that communion. The
relationship is unimpaired, but the powers of communion have inevitably suffered.

' To-day,' said Jesus, to the dying thief,—

answering for ever the objections of those who urge the impossibility of full forgiveness in the eleventh hour— ' thou shalt be with Me in Paradise.' At that moment the dying thief was restored to the relationship of a son. But that does not imply that he would be as able to enter into communion with his Father in the same degree as would have been possible if that relationship had never been broken. We, who have sinned, and been forgiven, know that the relationship is perfect. God's attitude to us is as though we had never sinned. But we know well enough ourselves that it was not without some kind of loss that we turned our back on Him. A soul born late into the kingdom is a *younger* son. A father may have many sons, but the elder can the more enter into communion with the father than those of five or six years old. The father's *relation* to them all is the same, but his communion with them is not the same. There must be growth on the part of the younger before the heights of communion which the elder enjoy can be reached. In the life after death, as here, that amount of communion will be possible which the spiritual capacity of the soul enables it to enjoy. The more we desire God, the more can we draw upon Him, and the more filled with meaning will communion with Him become; but the heights of communion will only be possible to those who, by long and patient endeavour, have become like Him.

To go back to our illustration. When that son came home to his father, broken in body and mind, the father would need to nurse him back again to health, mental and physical. And that process would

Condition of Life After Death

depend for its length on the amount of damage done. So when a man passes into the next world, a forgiven soul he may be, and he will be treated as such. He will be given all the rights and privileges which fall due to one who is a son. But certain processes will be necessary, painful processes, perhaps, before the effects of sin can be eradicated. But what a difference lies here, that to one who has reclaimed his position as a son those processes are in the nature of a friendly and helpful discipline, in which, though painful, he is glad to participate, knowing what they will bring. But to one who passes over entirely impenitent, they will be the hell of pain which he cannot perceive to be a cleansing fire, and though God is his Father, he prefers to think of Him as a magistrate, and himself, though a son for whom the arms of God are hungry, he prefers to consider as a criminal. It will be a long and painful process indeed before he can rise to communion with God. First must come a real penitence, then the acceptance of forgiveness, the purging of sin, and the long road which leads to greater and deeper communion, and boundless possibilities of progress.

V

Before the stage which we have called the consummation of the life after death can be reached, however, there must be, in certain cases, certain adjustments which we cannot but think will be made. There are those who have never heard of the Father of our Lord Jesus Christ, but they have lived up to the best light they had. They cannot be considered as suffering remorse save for that which they committed against the light they had. Indeed their great regret will be that Christian people did not make sure that the Gospel should be preached to them. The light they lived by was not consciously to them the light of Christ, perhaps, but they will see in another world, the authority which, all unconsciously, they obeyed, and they will know on whose strength, though unconsciously, they have rested during long years of honest effort. Growth, to them, when they ' see Jesus ' must surely in some way be speedy. Much will be counted to them for righteousness. They will in no way suffer, we can be sure, if they have responded to a conscience as enlightened as possible under difficult circumstances.

Those who have never had the light of reason; those who died in infancy, and those to whom the truth only appeared in a way so distorted that they could not accept it; to whom indeed it never seemed desirable because it was grievously misrepresented, or because the sincerity of the life did not lie behind the words of those who sought to teach it—to all these there will surely be such opportunity to develop the spiritual faculty as shall make them in no wise handicapped in the life after death. May we not say that He who conceivably preached to those spirits of the pre-Christian era in the prison bonds of ignorance, that they might not be the losers by circumstances outside their control[1]; He whose delight it was in the days of His flesh to give sight to blind eyes, will come to these in like condition who have passed into the further life spiritually blind, and with the same mercy, the same sympathy, the same healing power, touch their eyes and give them sight?

[1] Cf. 1 Peter iii 19.

CHAPTER V

The Consummation of the Life After Death

I

WE pass now to the blissful condition of the life after death, when the conditions described as hell and heaven are over. Heaven is no longer marred by the echoed pain of earth. No longer does the cry of man's anguish come up to God, for the earth life is a closed chapter in the history of humanity. Moreover hell no longer exists. For all, one imagines, the fires of remorse have done their healing work; the shame of spiritual disability no longer tortures; the memory of sin is that of an evil dream. At long last the prophecy is fulfilled that ' sorrow and sighing shall flee away.' As to whether memory has any final power to torture, we know ourselves that a point is reached when memories of evil, because of the memory of the amazing grace that has overcome that evil, have no longer any power to torture, for the memory of the evil lights up at once in the mind memories of the more than equal grace. Memories of child-losses and mistakes do not torture the adult. But perhaps only a poet can make adequate reply.

> Every evening, at set of sun,
> Silently stealing, one by one,
> Come the ships of the day that is done
> To the haven of memory.

After Death

Ships of pleasure and ships of pain,
Ships of losses and ships of gain:
In they glide from the mist and rain
Of the soul's unresting sea.

And here they anchor side by side,
And thus for a few brief hours abide;
Till, while they slumber, a stealthy tide
Comes silently in from the sea.

Then back to the infinite mist and the rain
Are swept the vessels of loss and pain;
And only the ships of pleasure remain
In the haven of memory!'

May it not be thus when the last evening falls, and the dawn that shall never be dimmed, nor ever end in sunset, shall herald the final victory of God?

We speak of this consummation because it seems to be the logical outcome of any intelligent thinking about God and the life after death. We do not pretend to be able to speculate about this final phase. It will mean, we believe, for all men, what poets and dreamers, saints and seers, have meant when they have spoken of the Beatific Vision. But what that means is difficult for the most daring imagination to conjecture. We cannot think of it as merely a kind of infinite adoration, since that involves the suppression of so many God-given faculties in our personality. We cannot conceive of it as service, for no service we can imagine remains to be done. We cannot conceive it as absorption into the Deity, for that means loss of individual personality and is little more attractive than annihilation.

Of our part then in the final consummation we cannot even hazard a guess. One thing we know. It

' Gilbert Thomas. ' The Haven of Memory,' from *Poems*: 1912-1919.

will be a fellowship worthy of God. We must leave it at that. And that is enough. Words which apply to all our thought of the after-life and which rebuke the too facile speculations of this book, certainly apply to the consummated life.

> My knowledge of that life is small,
>   The eye of faith is dim;
> But 'tis enough that Christ knows all,
>   And I shall be with Him.[1]

II

It is difficult to ascertain what is the place of the hope of the Second Coming in a consideration of the consummation of the life beyond. Indeed, in that it is a second coming to earth, it might be considered as beyond the scope of this discussion, but in that Christ is then conceived as re-entering heaven, no treatment, however brief and superficial, of the consummation of the life after death would be complete without it. We cannot dogmatically deny that Christ may come back to earth, manifested in some visible form with great power and glory, and that those then alive will be translated into the spirit world.[2]

Many of the older conceptions concerning the manner of His coming unfortunately suggest that Christ in His second advent will win the world by what we can but call theatrical and even forcible means, having failed to win it in the manner which has always been revealed as the ' ways of God to men,' namely, the way of patient and suffering love. And to speak

[1] Richard Baxter.   [2] Cf. Matt. xxiv. 31.

of the ' coming ' of One who is so amazingly ' here ' seems to introduce an anticlimax to present Christian experience. We shall make the attempt to find a conception more in harmony with what we know of Jesus.[1] ' His kingdom is of the spirit and He would not coerce the moral judgement by any display of a power which belongs to another realm of values.'[2]

III

In the first place the suggestion ought not to be omitted that Jesus Himself may have expected the Second Coming to be much sooner, and even within a few years of His own Ascension. May it not have been that if men's faith and enthusiasm had been all that Jesus confidently expected, the Coming would have been speedily possible? Christ's promises were relative to faith. Only faith could accomplish the fulfilment. We cannot say what might have happened had human faith been more potent. Christ might have visibly come, as Paul first expected, within his own lifetime. We cannot but think that the long delay has its cause with humanity rather than with God.[3]

On the other hand it may be that at the end of the age there will be some special manifestation of Christ and of His power.[4] ' There will be,' says Prof. H. R.

[1] For a discussion of the language ascribed to Jesus concerning the Second Coming, see Appendix II, p. 169.

[2] Prof. W. F. Howard in *The Modern Churchman*, July 1923.

[3] See Hogg. *Christ's Message of the Kingdom*, pp. 96-7. Cf. Mackintosh. *Immortality and the Future*. Footnote, pp 130-1.

[4] Believers in a millenium hold that Christ will come and reign on earth for a thousand years. The belief is based on a single passage in the Apocalypse (xx. 1-10), which is interpreted literally. It is very doubtful as to whether any numeral in the Revelation is to be literally interpreted. Such interpretation is the crudest kind of exegesis.

Consummation of Life After Death

Mackintosh, ' a final manifestation of His supremacy in a mode recognizable by all, and exhibiting the last issues of the divine redemptive rule of all things in heaven and earth. It is no primitive fanaticism, it is part of believing hope towards God, to expect a real close of history, a worthy *dénouement* of the story of a world in which God had redeemed His people.'[1]

As to what the mode of that manifestation will be we cannot say. It will not be a display calculated to awe and terrify the world into submission. The ' blood and fire and vapour of smoke ' so often thought of as part of the stage scenery of a second coming are merely the apocalyptic dress which such thought wore in Jewish imaginations. But whatever it may be, it will be a manifestation which is in harmony with what we know of Jesus, and with what we know of His methods of appealing to, and of winning mankind. It may take the form of some great movement spreading silently and swiftly like some glorious infection, in which men everywhere will be constrained to crown Him as the King of their lives. No outward show, no visible ' coming ' would be more relevant, effective, or more after His heart than that, for His Kingdom is not an earthly kingdom : it is a kingdom of human hearts.

Nor is it unimportant to remember the sense in which Jesus is always coming.[2] In the hour of death ; in the moment of a great decision for right ; in the

---

[1] Mackintosh. *Immortality and the Future*, p. 140.

[2] Jesus is for ever coming again, not in physical horror, but in moral triumph; not in convulsions of nature, but in conversion of heart; not in the ghastly melodrama of a dissolving universe, but in the still small voice of conscience and in the silent growth of love.' Dr. Momerie. *Immortality*, p. 98.

95

choice of a high ideal; in the determination of some
great resolve, Jesus comes to human hearts. He comes
to us in the stranger seeking shelter, in the lonely
breaking heart that comes to us for comfort, in the
little child who seeks our love; and he who will
minister to such, finds Advent imminent indeed, for
he may celebrate it in his heart.

IV

The ultimate triumph of Love. The teaching of
Scripture, our own reason, and our knowledge of what
God is, demand that we should posit that finally God
will be victorious in His long designs for the children
of men, and this without any violation of the sanctity
of the free will of the human personality. It is inconceivable to the Christian that God can fail ultimately, however stubborn man may be. It is impossible
to think that the Cross of Christ, and all that that
must involve—far more than we at present know—is
inadequate to draw all men to the heart of humanity's
greatest Lover. And the way of escape from this
conclusion surely does not lie through the assumption
of a hell in which souls are forced to acknowledge the
supremacy of Love. A forced confession would surely
not be ' to the glory of God the Father.'[1] One soul
in such a hell would mar the victory and make it
incomplete and unsatisfactory. It would mean that
God could only attain supremacy by stooping to use
means unworthy of men, much less of the Divine
Creator.

[1] See Phil. ii. 10-12.

Consummation of Life After Death

This failure of God ' would mean the eternal enthronement of the devil and the powers of evil over one half of God's dominion. It would mean the perpetuation of sin, hatred, lawlessness and defiance of God. It would mean practically a huge divine failure and defeat in the great conflict of the ages. It would mean dualism of the most humiliating and revolting kind, and it becomes increasingly difficult to understand how and why the Church through so many centuries has entertained, and even fiercely clung to, such a moral impossibility or to such a meagre measuring of God's final triumph.'[1]

New Testament writers do not seem to hesitate even to revel in the idea of a final complete victory. It is the keynote of at least one of Paul's epistles.[2] Paul speaks of the ' exceeding greatness of his power . . . according to that working of the strength of his might which he wrought in Christ, when he raised him from the dead and made him to sit at his right hand in the heavenly places, far above all rule, and authority, and power, and dominion, and every name that is named, not only in this world, but also in that which is to come : and he put all things in subjection under his feet, and gave him to be head over all things.'[3] ' He *must* reign ' we are told again ' till he hath put all his enemies under his feet.'[4] And that ' God highly exalted him, and gave unto him the name which is above every name; that in the name of Jesus every knee should bow, and every tongue confess that

[1] J. G. Greenhough. *The Last Things.*

[2] Ephesians.   [3] Eph. i. 19-22.   [4] 1 Cor. xv. 25.

After Death

Jesus Christ is Lord to the glory of God the Father.'[1]

And Paul has the highest authority for these and kindred statements. 'I,' said Jesus, 'if I be lifted up from the earth, will draw *all* men unto myself '[2]; and in the parables of the lost sheep and the lost coin, the significant phrases are used ' until he find it,' ' until she find it.'[3] One cannot help feeling that he who will not receive the idea of Christ's final victory must find some way of explaining this idea so strongly rooted in Christian thought from the beginning, and so strongly in accordance with what our conception of God would lead us to expect. He ' willeth that *all* men should be saved,'[4] and the prayer of Christ, which He taught the world to pray, will not for ever remain unanswered; ' Thy will be done.'[5]

Thinkers and poets have always clung to this idea. Says Prof. William James ' Most religious men believe (or ' know,' if they be mystical) that not only they themselves, but the whole universe of beings to whom God is present, are secure in His parental hands. There is a sense, a dimension, they are sure, in which we are *all* saved, in spite of the gates of hell and all adverse terrestrial appearances. God's existence is the guarantee of an ideal order that shall be permanently preserved. This world may indeed, as science assures us, some day burn up or freeze; but if it is part of His order the old ideals are sure to be brought elsewhere to fruition, so that where God is, tragedy is only provisional and partial, and shipwreck and disso-

---

[1] Phil. ii. 10-12. [2] John xii. [3] Luke xv. 5 and 8. [4] 1 Tim. ii. 4.
[5] See also 1 Tim. 4. 10; Col. i. 19-20; Eph. i. 10.

Consummation of Life After Death

lution are not the absolutely final things.'[1] ' It is incredible,' says Leckie in his recent Kerr Lectures, ' that God has bestowed on any creature the power to perpetuate evil and work its own everlasting misery. Such an endowment would not be a good gift, and all the gifts of God are good.'[2] In similar strain the Lady Margaret Professor of Divinity at Cambridge, lecturing at King's College, London University, said, ' The Christian conception of God does not allow even one per cent. of failures—it is not enough to have ninety-nine sheep out of the flock of a hundred, safe in the fold. It does not admit of the extinction either of an incipient, or of a stunted or warped or ill-grown personality. It requires that all should come to the measure of the stature of the fulness of Christ. . . The new life must offer a new start. . . . Our affections and will demand final universal restoration . . . if the imperative demand of the affections and the will is finally baulked, then indeed man can conceive a good higher than reality, and the creature would have outgrown the Creator.'[3]

The greatest exponent of this gospel in literature is Tennyson.

> The wish, that of the living whole
>   No life may fail beyond the grave,
>   Derives it not from what we have
> The likest God within the soul?
>
> Oh yet we trust that somehow good
>   Will be the final goal of ill.

. . . . .

[1] Prof. William James. *Varieties of Religious Experience*, p. 517.

[2] Leckie. *Op. cit.*, p. 275.

[3] J. F. Bethune-Baker. King's College Lectures on ' Immortality.' (University of London Press), p. 37-8.

After Death

That nothing walks with aimless feet;
  That not one life shall be destroy'd,
  Or cast as rubbish to the void,
When God hath made the pile complete.

     .   .   .   .   .

Behold, we know not anything;
  I can but trust that good shall fall
  At last—far off—at last, to all,
And every winter change to spring.[1]

We might fill many pages with similar quotations. Repeatedly in Browning, Tennyson, Cowper, Whittier, Whitman, Longfellow—poets who are to us something of what the prophets of old were to the Jews—we may find definitely stated the conviction that

God by God's ways occult
May, doth, I will believe, bring back
All wanderers to a single track.[2]

V

It has sometimes been claimed that the Gospel of God's final victory, denying as it does the possibility of an endless hell, would, if widely preached, lessen the force of the Evangelical appeal. But to preach the gospel of Christ as a means of escaping possible unpleasantness in the next world is surely a low ideal for the preacher. That gospel first and foremost is a power which redeems and transforms a man's life and makes it worth living in this world. The appeal to fear alone we feel is rightly out of date and its use should be deprecated. Men who appear to be won by it are won unfairly if they are really won at all. And

[1] Tennyson. *In Memoriam*, liv.-lv.
[2] See also *The Afterworld of the Poets*.

for the preacher—with however important a sense of his own mission—to feel that another human being, or set of human beings, depends absolutely for final salvation on his proclamation of the gospel, seems to give him an importance which we can hardly allow in any individual.

Let us preach by all means to the utmost of our power, for even from the point of view of the life after death we give a soul who accepts the Gospel an enormous uplift in the fight for character. Christ is the Ideal of the human personality, and by no other way may a man attain to ideal human life so speedily as by acceptance of Him, here and now. But let us not do God the injustice of imagining that those whom we could not touch will be eternally handicapped. Surely they will have a ' first chance ' to make good in the spirit-world. It is too great a responsibility for any man if another's final destiny depends on him.

Also it must be said that goodness is not lessened by our assertion of its final triumph. Nor is sin strengthened because we assert its final defeat. The certainty of punishment we do not deny for a moment. We hold, moreover, that it will vary directly with sin committed in this life. Indeed, the whole question of the final victory of God seems remote enough; so remote that if rightly understood, it can in any case influence but little the preaching of to-day. And the preacher's message cannot be strengthened in the long run by an appeal which lessens our conception of God. A conscience may be temporarily stirred by an appeal to the fear of an endless punishment, but if that conscience cannot acknowledge such a threat to be either just or moral, the effect of the appeal is necessarily short-lived, and, indeed, may more than likely repel a man, and turn him from a Father so caricatured.

'It is incorrect,' says Prof. Mackintosh, 'to say that even unquestioning acceptance of universal restitution must weaken a man's zeal for the Christian propaganda. Very probably it has done so in certain cases as extreme forms of Calvinism did. But we need only recall names like Erskine of Linlathen, Crossley of Manchester, Blumhardt in Germany—all convinced universalists but also active promoters of evangelism— to feel that as a whole the charge is sweeping and unjust. These men, if we are to credit their own story, felt a deeper zest in service due to the new hope.'[1]

VI

Will any one be finally lost? We know that God 'desireth not the death of a sinner but rather that he should turn from his wickedness and live,' but may not that desire in some extreme cases be frustrated? We have suggested already that the conditions of heaven and hell must give the possibility of growth so that the most abandoned will have a chance of self improvement and of growing towards the light. Another possibility emerges. Man, if his personality remains the same, must still retain a free will. Supposing even in another would he refuses the light, what then?

Let us admit at once that the possibility is unlikely

[1] Mackintosh. *Op cit.*, p. 206.

in the extreme. In the life after death spiritual values, as we have said, will not only be, but will be seen to be supreme. Therefore growth of spiritual capacity will be the only possibility of happiness, and this surely the spirit will realize. Again, such a refusal as is contemplated, would mean—to express it in figurative language—that men so hate goodness, that, in all the light and knowledge of that other land, when they see Christ more clearly than ever before, when they know Him for what He is, and know what He has wrought for them if they will accept it, when they are even held in His embrace, they raise their hand, and smite the Compassionate Face. When one increasingly realizes the ' good in the worst of us,' one feels that that great refusal will not in one single instance be made.

But we must face the possibility. What would be the ultimate destiny of such ? The answer probably is that finally such a soul would cease to be a personality. ' We keep open,' says a modern theologian, ' the solemn possibility that final dissolution will be the ultimate end for such souls as have completely lost the power to recognize and desire goodness, and respond to the love of God.'[1] The wages of sin, long continued without repentance, is death; the death of the soul. The two laws mentioned in a previous chapter, which we called the laws of atrophy and porosis, have, as their logical issue, unless the processes are interrupted by other laws, that same dark tragedy, the death of a soul. Men who have continued in sin so long that

---

[1] C. W. Emmet, *Immortality*, p. 216.

the soul lives in a darkness of its own creation, which
it has even learned to love, and which, passing into
the next life, still hates the light, and delights in its
own blindness, cannot be regarded as necessarily immortal. He who brought it into being may cause that
existence to cease, or a least to cease as a conscious
and separate personality, and to sink back into that
bottomless cosmic ' mind-pool ' from which we were
all drawn as water from a well.

The New Testament seems also to recognize this
possibility. There is an unforgivable sin—' to call
the highest manifestation of the Holy Ghost, devilry,'
to resist His pleadings however often they may be
advanced, to resist His love with open eyes, choosing
always evil instead of good, choosing even in the
radiance of eternity the darkness rather than the light,
until the pleadings can be heard no more, and ' the
light that lighteth every man coming into the world '
has become darkness in the soul. He who commits
that sin unrepentingly can find ' no forgiveness either
in this world or in that which is to come.'[1]

The burning of the tares which suggests their
utter destruction (Matt. xiii. 40) and the burning of
the unfruitful vine (John xv. 6) seem to indicate the
possibility of a final dissolution of individuality.[2] The
author of the letter to the Hebrews contemplates the
same possibility. ' If we sin wilfully after that we
have received the knowledge of the truth '—and that
knowledge must come fully only in the life after death
—' there remaineth no more a sacrifice for sins, but

[1] Matt. xii. 32; Mark iii. 29; Luke xii. 10.
[2] Cf. also 2 Thess. i. 6-9; John iii. 36.

Consummation of Life After Death

a certain fearful expectation of judgement, and a fierceness of fire which shall *devour* the adversaries.'[1]

The most terrible words of all were spoken by the gentlest Lips in the world. ' Be not afraid of them which kill the body, but are not able to kill the soul : but rather fear him which is able to destroy both soul and body in hell.'[2] To our mind the *possibility* is absolutely stated of final dissolution for those whose character is all wood, hay, stubble; the things which the cleansing fires will not purge but utterly destroy. ' Final ruin,' says Bishop Gore, ' may involve, I cannot but think, such a dissolution of personality as carries with it the cessation of personal consciousness. In this way the final ruin of irretrievably lost spirits, awful as it is to contemplate, may be found consistent with St. Paul's anticipation of a universe in which ultimately God is to be all in all—which does not seem to be really compatible with the existence of a region of everlastingly tormented and rebellious spirits.'[3]

VII

We turn now from the New Testament which admits the possibility; we turn from an expression which speaks of a spirit as ' irretrievably lost,' and

[1] Heb. x. 26-7.

[2] Matt. x. 28 and Luke xii 4. The question arises as to whether the Evangelists allowed the current Jewish eschatology unduly to influence them even when they recorded the alleged words of Jesus. It is difficult to accept the argument that Jesus took over the conceptions of God in Jewish eschatology *in toto*, since His whole teaching is as different from the teaching we find in ' The Book of Enoch,' ' The Apocalypse of Baruch,' ' Ecclesiasticus,' and kindred books, as light is from darkness. See the whole argument of *The Lord of Thought*, Dougall and Emmet.

[3] *Immortality*, p. 92ff.

we look again at the character of God. An annihilated soul is a lost soul after all. And God is the Father of all souls. Will He be content with a victory which has necessitated the cessation of the consciousness even of one? The man who repels us because of our narrow vision, is dear to Him; dear as the worst son of a family is dear to a real father-heart. ' He calleth them all by name.' He knows all humanity not as a crowd but as individuals. The Eternal Heart is not like a War Office where men are known by a number. God is a Father who knows and yearns over the most degraded of His children. As a logical possibility, if the light of God in the human soul is entirely quenched, we may hold a belief in annihilation. But is it ever entirely quenched? When it appears so to us, it may not be so to God. When a man himself may think so, God may see the last tiny flickering spark, and fan it to a flame again.

> Beneath the veriest ash there hides a spark of soul
> Which, quickened by love's breath may yet pervade the whole
> O' the grey, and free again be fire.[1]
>
> .　　.　　.　.
>
> Thou lovest all: Thy erring child may be
> Lost to himself, but never lost to Thee!
>
> ＊　　＊　＊　　＊
>
> Wilt Thou not make, Eternal Source and Goal,
> In Thy long years, life's broken circle whole,
> And change to praise the cry of a lost soul?[2]

We have read somewhere of the leader of a great orchestra who was reported to have such a sensitive

[1] Browning ' Fifine.'
[2] Whittier. *The Cry of a Lost Soul.*

Consummation of Life After Death

ear that, if one player played a wrong note, he knew, and the discord jarred upon him. And if a single player stopped playing he knew, and the harmony was incomplete to the master ear. God is like that. We have spoken of a possibility. It is well that we should keep it before us. We believe it to be a very dim one. Finally in the great consummation not one note will create a discord, nor will a single player be missing when that great harmony resounds through the courts of heaven acclaiming the last unending victory of God. In our best moments such is the victory which we ourselves should desire; such is the victory we should achieve if all the methods known as Infinite Power and Love were open to us. Will God's ultimate achievement be something less than the highest human desire?

Be that as it may. Keep that possibility who will. There is one thing which we hold to be beyond doubt; one thing which admits of no alternative. The great Seeker of souls will never sit down on the right hand of the throne of God in the consummation of His glory, while there is one coin *which still bears the image and superscription of the King,* lying in the dust hidden and forgotten; nor while there is one sheep *who still is not too deaf to hear the Shepherd's voice,* far out on the cold dark mountains, friendless and alone.

CHAPTER VI

Our Present Relation to Those Who Have Passed to the Life After Death

I

WHAT is to be our relation to those whom we call the dead? The story of the witch of Endor who called up the spirit of Samuel to be consulted by Saul,[1] shows the antiquity of the desire to commune with the dead. This desire has been manifested in various ways ever since. But is the Christian to indulge in spiritualistic practices? In his book, *The New Revelation*, Sir Arthur Conan Doyle claims that such practices are definitely Christian. The events of the Transfiguration of our Lord are to him the events of a spiritualistic materialization. Peter, James, and John, formed the psychic circle.[2] He also dogmatically states that the early Christians practised Spiritualism,[3] and that the gifts which Paul enumerates as being the necessary equipment for the Christian disciple,[4] are ' simply the list of the gifts of a very

[1] 1 Sam. xxviii. 7ff.
[2] Sir Arthur Conan Doyle. *The New Revelation*, pp. 79-80.
[3] *Ib.*, p. 123. [4] I. Cor. xii. 8-11.

powerful medium.'[1]   When claims like these are made, the attitude of Christianity to the whole subject must be stated.

Spiritualism was never more popular than it is to-day.   One reason of this is the widespread bereavement caused by the greatest war the world has ever known.   It is not unnatural that hearts stung by sorrow should seek knowledge of what has happened, and what is still happening, to their dead. It is not unnatural that they should seek to commune with them.   And it must be admitted, that the dangerous popularity of spiritualistic inquiry among unqualified and unscientific seekers, is largely due to the hesitancy of modern Christian thought fearlessly to pronounce its views on the subject of the life after death; especially that part of the subject dealing with the relation between the living and the dead.   This hesitancy has meant a failure to give positive comfort to hearts utterly weary of mere negations, half-truths, or dogmas which, however rigidly and repeatedly presented, do not bear the impress of either truth or sincerity.

A second reason for this popularity is that the subject has been dragged out of the half-lights which have shrouded it in the past; and has, as far as is possible, been scientifically stated.   Moreover men whose names demand that they should be given a respectful hearing can now be quoted to substantiate spiritualistic claims.   The influence, on English speak-

[1] *The New Revelation,* p. 80

After Death

ing people, of Sir Oliver Lodge and Sir Arthur Conan Doyle is probably most potent.[1]

II

These facts—the new popularity, the new importance, and the new spirit of inquiry—should cause the Christian thought of the world fairly to state its position and its attitude.

On careful investigation of the phenomena we find something in the conclusions of spiritualistic inquiry which is in harmony with modern thought concerning the life after death. The present writer was amazed to find on reading *The New Revelation* much that he had come to accept as truth concerning the life after death, though, of course, arrived at in a totally different way.

Perhaps the following may be quoted as illustrating this similarity in certain directions. ' Hell as a permanent place does not exist. But the idea of punishment, of purifying chastisement, in fact of purgatory, is justified by reports from the other side. Without such punishment there could be no justice in the Universe, for how impossible it would be to imagine that the fate of a Rasputin is the same as that of a Father Damien. The punishment is very certain and very serious though in its less severe forms

[1] It is not in any spirit of hostility to the great service which both these writers have done to clear thinking on the subject of Spiritualism, to point out for the warning of the reader that the authority of Sir Oliver Lodge and Sir Arthur Conan Doyle is greater on questions of science and literature than of communication with the dead. Ability in one direction does not *ipso facto* mean authority to speak in another.

it only consists in the fact that the grosser souls are in lower spheres with a knowledge that their own deeds have placed them there, but also with the hope that expiation and the help of those above them, will educate them and bring them level with the others. In this saving process the higher spirits find part of their employment.'[1] ' Reports from the other world are all agreed as to the pleasant condition of life in the beyond. They agree that like goes to like, that all who love or who have interests in common are united . . . that they would by no means desire to return.'[2] ' Communications usually come from those who have not long passed over and tend to grow fainter, as one would expect.'[3] The explanation of this is that a spirit rises to a higher life and is thus further away from the earth life. ' All agree that life beyond is for a limited period after which they pass on to yet other phases . . . the lower cannot ascend, but the higher can descend at will.' ' It is pre-eminently a life of the mind as this is of the body. Preoccupations of food, money, lust, pain, &c., are of the body and are gone. Music, the arts, intellectual and spiritual knowledge and progress have increased . . . thought is the medium of conversation.'[4] ' The newly passed do not know they are dead, and it is a very long time before they can be made to understand it.'[5]

These quotations cannot be said to be out of harmony with modern speculation concerning life after

[1] Conan Doyle, *Op. cit.*, p. 90-1.

[2] *Ib.*, p. 91.　[3] *Ib.*, p. 95.　[4] *Ib.*, pp. 96-8.　[5] *Ib.*, pp. 100-1.

death but the good grain is still very much mixed with chaff. Has not this always been the difficulty in regard to this subject? Some intelligible communication will be in process of interpretation through table tapping when suddenly it will be discovered that some one is rocking it with his foot or with an appliance. How many mediums have been found fraudulent— even after a certain amount of *bona fide* work—and dismissed! Sir Arthur Conan Doyle admits that he has had to get rid of many for this reason, though it does not seem clear that he has regarded their work previous to exposure as untrustworthy! Mr. Joseph McCabe fills pages of his book, *Is Spiritualism based on Fraud?* with instances of the detection and exposure of fraudulent mediums. That is the great difficulty to the average man. It is not that he is unduly prejudiced. It is that in the past the whole subject has been such a mixture of truth (for he feels that there is some truth behind it) and falsehood, the possible and the impossible, the serious and the grotesquely silly, that the one cannot be separated from the other. And unfortunately that difficulty still remains.[1]

But apart from the fact of this mixture there is, to the untrained investigator, a dangerous element in spiritualism. Sir Oliver Lodge himself gives a very serious warning to those who might be tempted to dabble in Spiritualism by reading his and kindred books. ' There is,' he says,—and especially must this be true of those in profound grief or of a nervous and

[1] See Appendix III.

excitable temperament—'a terrible danger of the dabbler losing his own self-control.' Another well-known writer, himself an expert in mental disease,[1] who wrote a strong criticism of *Raymond*, interprets those words. They mean that there is a very serious danger of the unscientific explorer losing his reason, or at the very least becoming the pathetic subject of fits of hysteria or profound melancholy.

The point seems important enough to warrant the quotation from *Raymond* in full. 'It may be asked, do I recommend all bereaved persons to devote the time and attention which I have done to getting communications and recording them? Most certainly I do not. I am a student of the subject, and a student often undertakes detailed labour of a special kind. I reecommend people in general to learn and realize that their loved ones are still active and useful and interested and happy—more alive than ever in one sense—and to make up their minds to live a useful life till they rejoin them.'[2]

In speaking of the conclusion that there is some-thing evil and dangerous in Spiritualism we cannot rule out the possibility that unembodied evil intelli-gences both exist and are at work. The contention made by Spiritualists that mediums are required *on both sides* seems to leave a communication open to diabolical interference. Some will recall Tennyson's conversation with Longfellow. Tennyson explains the phenomena by supposing the existence of ' Pucks.' Such a suggestion seems a fitting explanation of much

[1] Dr. Charles Mercier in *Spiritualism and Sir Oliver Lodge*.
[2] *Raymond*, p. 225.

that is grotesque in communications alleged to be received from the dead. At the same time it is a suggestion which makes little appeal to the modern mind. To explain one set of phenomena, another is brought in more inexplicable still, and belief in evil spirits is discarded more and more as man's thought progresses.

There is something unconvincing in the claims of Spiritualism. Ruling out for the moment the possibility of fraud, the whole claim of spiritualists is discounted in the minds of many earnest seekers after truth because it does not seem impossible that the science of telepathy—the action of mind on mind, and mind on matter—will be able to account for a great many of the phenomena. It is too much to say at present that telepathy can disprove the spiritualistic hypothesis, for the very word ' telepathy ' is a label for ignorance rather than a scientific term, but it is possible that in many cases it can already offer an alternative solution. Nor does it seem too much to suggest that when the knowledge of telepathic influence is further explored and reduced to a science, an explanation of all so called spiritualistic phenomena may be available.

Take an instance quoted by Prof. William Brown, the famous psychologist, psycho-therapist, and neurologist to the Fourth Army of the B.E.F. in France, in his lecture on ' Immortality in the Light of Modern Psychology.'[1] ' If a patient is hypnotized and then it is suggested to him that he can see things

[1] p. 160.

happening at home, he will readily relate what he appears to see. He will see his wife writing a letter, will be able to read what she writes, will, as though in a dream, be able to pass from room to room, and when he wakes up will be quite certain that he has been at home. Sometimes what he sees will be what is actually happening, but often the patient sees something which has not happened at all. The patient's mind has become so suggestible that the thought of home suggests certain characteristic happenings of home life, and then, working on these, the mind improvises as it goes along.' We must surely compare such a statement with the so called ' visions ' of mediums. Pathological psychology has not yet spoken the final word by any means on much evidence claimed to prove that spiritualistic forces are at work.

Again when a sitter in a séance asks a question, he must in almost every case have in his mind some idea of the nature of the answer he expects. The medium who is in a trance makes a reply. How are we to be sure that the questioner does not impress the psychically sensitive mind of the medium with that answer? That might easily happen with both sitter and medium unconscious of that mental coercion. Both may be entirely *bona fide* and honest in their search, and yet be deceived into thinking a result is due to spiritualistic forces, when it is simply due to telepathy. Again and again a medium makes an answer, which, in the ordinary state could not have been made because of ignorance, yet we do know that the subconscious mind exerts itself to a remarkable degree, and it seems unnecessary to postulate the communication of the spirits of the dead.

Dr. Mitchell establishes the possibility (which Baudouin reached along a different line) that the ' controls ' with which mediums claim intercourse may be their own ' secondary ' (dissociated) personalities.[1]

The poet Coleridge relates a case[2] where a servant maid in the fever of delirium quoted long passages of Hebrew and Greek, of both of which languages she was entirely ignorant. Inquiries showed that she had previously been in the service of a minister who used to walk up and down his little garden reciting passages in these languages. They had been frequently audible to her, and her subconscious memory had registered them, and in an abnormal state she produced them. She could not have been a normal person psychically, but neither is the professional medium. It is indeed a wise rule which says that supernatural methods are not to be assumed until natural causes have been ruled out.

Perhaps another case may be quoted from an essay on ' The Mind and the Brain ' by Capt. J. A. Hadfield, a well-known psychologist. ' In a series of séances arranged by the Society for Psychical Research, with Mrs. Piper as medium, the investigators sought to obtain an account of a certain conversation which took place between Mrs. Sidgwick and Mr. F. W. H. Myers some time before his death. This conversation was known to none except to the two participants. In

[1] Cf. *Christianity and Psychology.* Barry, p. 172.
[2] Quoted in *Spiritualism and Sir Oliver Lodge.* Mercier.

ner trance Mrs. Piper claimed to have access to Myers and an attempt was made to induce the spirit of Myers to reproduce the conversation through Mrs. Piper. As long as Mrs. Sidgwick was absent and did not come into contact with Mrs. Piper, the medium failed to reproduce the conversation. When, however, Mrs. Sidgwick came into contact with Mrs. Piper, there was a remarkable, though not perfectly accurate, account given of the conversation. That is to say, it was the proximity of Mrs. Sidgwick, who *knew the conversation*, that made the difference. Mrs. Sidgwick, therefore, concludes, and rightly so in my opinion, that the medium became possessed of the information not from the spirit of " Myers," but by mental transference from Mrs. Sidgwick herself. In other words though it did not prove communication with the spirit world it did afford important evidence of telepathy."[1]

III

To the Christian then, it seems that the conclusion of the matter is this. We find in Spiritualism something that impresses us as containing the truth. There must be some reality behind all the phenomena. Sir William Barrett has claimed little more than we already believe when he says, ' No candid student of the evidence can, in my opinion, resist the conclusion that there exists an unseen world of intelligent beings some of whom have striven to prove with more or less success that they once lived on earth.' With that moderate

Immortality, p 55.

claim we are in total agreement. At the same time
there is certainly much in the phenomena presented,
which cannot yet be accepted by the normal Christian
as being a revelation of the nature of life beyond the
grave. To him this part of the evidence seems at best
grotesque in the extreme, and at variance with any
Christian view of the nature of life after death. It
must emphatically be stated that up to the present,
Spiritualism has not made a single definite, valuable,
or original contribution to Christian thought concerning that life. At the same time surely the Christian
is to keep an open mind and certainly is not to write
the whole subject down as being un-Christian. Truth
of great and permanent value may yet come through
these channels. It may yet be that research in this
direction will make for the definite enrichment of the
Christian experience, for instance, in the matter of
prayer. We dare not shut any door through which
truth may come.

In the meantime the Christian must be content to
leave such inquiries to experts. He has in his own faith
a heritage, which, if more fully explored, will give to
him more than all that is supplied for his comfort and
encouragement by modern spiritualism. Let him ask
himself whether he knows all the values of prayer as
described in the New Testament, of quiet thought about
those who have gone, of that great experience which
the Church has called ' the Communion of saints.'
He will find therein more healthy food than the séance
will ever give to him. And he will avoid its dangers,
and its frequent absurdities.

To Those Who Have Passed

IV

Prayer for the Dead.

And answer made King Arthur breathing hard:
' My end draws nigh . . .
    . . . but thou,
If thou should'st never see my face again,
Pray for my soul. More things are wrought by prayer
Than this world dreams of ' . . .[1]

That same wistful longing not to lose sight of the dead altogether, and the continued interest of bereaved persons in the lives of those whom for the time being they had lost, led to the practice of prayer for the dead. This practice is condemned in many quarters. It is doubtless true that the Roman Catholic Church has frightened Protestants from it, by the superstition and unreality with which it is there surrounded. This is true concerning the dogma of Purgatory as we have seen. But in the simple practice of prayer for the dead there is nothing which can be condemned on Christian grounds.

Sir Oliver Lodge has a passage that is very pertinent. In *Raymond*[2] he says, ' For those who believe in prayer at all to cease from praying for the welfare of their friends because they are materially inaccessible —though perhaps spiritually more accessible than before—is to succumb unduly to the residual evil of past ecclesiastical abuses, and to lose an opportunity of happy service.'

I have read somewhere of a little child who was rebuked for praying to her father who had recently

---

[1] Tennyson. *Morte d'Arthur.*   [2] p. 367.

died. She said afterwards that she felt that a door had been slammed in her face, shutting the loved one for ever from her. It is that ' door ' that ought never to be shut, particularly in the hour of bereavement. To shut it is to place the world of spirits far away and far removed from our life. Some of the greatest saints known to the present writer have not only prayed for the departed, but have themselves lived in the spirit-world, with their loved ones real and near. They have prayed with them, as well as for them. A visitor would imagine that the one who had passed over was, at furthest, merely in the next room. To be able to do that is to conquer the sense of separation which is so often the most poignant part of bereavement.

It has been claimed that prayer for the dead is unnecessary, since the persons prayed for are in a special sense with God, and beyond the reach of prayer. But we refuse to accept the phrase ' beyond the reach of prayer ' as being true of any conscious personality. And if the word ' necessary ' is to be employed in its strict sense, it must be admitted that the same argument holds true on this side of the grave. Our friends here are with God. Prayer is not *necessary* for them. They will not be struck with disease, or death, or damnation, because we do not pray for them. Otherwise we should never dare to be off our knees; otherwise every war mourner might torture herself with the thought that if only she had prayed more, her beloved would have been saved from German bullets and shells. No! Rather do we know that we can exercise a loving and helpful ministry. We are not guided by what

To Those Who Have Passed

is necessary either to the living or the dead. Prayer is an act of faith in God's love. We release His power into other lives. Why should that close with death?

Again, If I pray for a man I establish at once a link with that man's life. Why should that link be broken by death? He is still the same human personality. We have tried to show that even the set of experiences which we have called heaven are not wholly blissful. Is it no help to those on the other side to have the benefit of the prayerful sympathy of loved ones on this? And if, in the fires of remorse, character is being re-shaped, is it nothing that prayer is being offered that the cleansing may avail for holiness at long last?

Writing of prayer for the dead, the authoress of *Pro Christo et Ecclesia* says, ' It behoves us to commit our relations to them entirely to God. Have we care concerning them? Are we not told to cast all our care on God? Have we desires on their behalf? Is not the Apostle's exhortation sound to lay all our desires before God? Do we long unspeakably to have our sense of blank ignorance and loss changed to some richer faith and nobler comfort? Have we not the promise that to ask is to receive, to seek is to find, and to knock is to have some door opened? It is probable that we cannot do a thing more foolish, more detrimental to ourselves, more grieving to God, than to cherish any desire or doubt, hope or fear, that we do not confide to His attention and help. If this is done with frankness, and with affiance in the Divine love, we may know that to each may come that feeling and faith concerning those in the other world which will lead to right action. If it is possible that those we have loved and lost from sight can aid and refresh us, we shall experience this. If those we love are in need of our help, being still holden with the chain of their sins, we shall be moved to give that help. . . . The true religious life would seem to imply direct prayer to God for departed souls.'[1]

To be perfectly frank with ourselves is to admit that we all pray for the dead. We do so every time we pray for the Church of Christ. We do so when bereavement falls upon us. We do it unconsciously. Our thoughts follow the loved one. We cannot help thinking, wondering, hoping. Such thoughts are the very essence of prayer. Would we have the mother forget her son killed in action? Whether we would or no, such forgetfulness is impossible. And some of us are beginning to find language for such thoughts, refusing to be frightened by abuses of the past, believing that there is a gracious and kindly ministry, too long neglected, to be rendered by prayers for the dead, and perhaps a mutual helpfulness,—who knows? —by their prayers for us. Men who have never lost, or whose minds are set in a certain mould may indeed forbid it. Those who have lost, and who dare to follow a helpful light, will hesitate not one whit, for all the rules of theology. To them it will not be unnatural to speak with the Father concerning those in the bosom of His care.

[1] *Concerning Prayer*, p. 496.

To Those Who Have Passed

V

There is a whole gospel touching our relation with our dead which has sunk below the horizon of our religious thinking. Thus to let it sink is to lose a real link with those whom ' we have loved and lost awhile.' Moreover it contains a reply to the charge that Spiritualism fulfils a need unmet by Christianity. In the Creed this gospel is stated very briefly : ' I believe in the Communion of Saints.' We mean by the expression, a communion of those still in the body with one another, *and with those who have ' passed through the body and gone.'* And generally speaking the phrase implies the latter rather than the former. The word ' communion ' is a happy one. The highest communion of all is one without words because it is above words. Here the Christian, it seems to us, rises far above the spiritualist. The latter demands communication. The former is content with communion. And communion is higher, closer, more intimate than communication. Communion is a fellowship, spirit with spirit.

> I watch thee from the quiet shore,
>   Thy spirit up to mine can reach,
>   But in dear words of human speech
> We two communicate no more.'

' God forbid,' says S. Augustine writing of S. Monica, his mother, after her death ; ' God forbid that in a higher state of existence she should cease to think of me, to long to comfort me, she who loved me more than words can tell.'

[1] Tennyson. *In Memoriam.* lxxxv.

After Death

In his recent *Outspoken Essays* Dean Inge writes as follows : ' A few highly educated men, who have long been playing with occultism, and gratifying their intellectual curiosity by exploring the dark places of perverted mysticism, have been swept off their feet by it, and their authority as " men of science " has dispelled the hesitation of many more to accept what they dearly wished to believe. It will be said that there is scientific evidence for survival. This claim is now made. Cases are reported with much parade of scientific language and method, and those who reject the stories with contemptuous incredulity are accused of mere prejudice. . . . It is no doubt just possible that among the vibrations of the fundamental ingredients of our world—those attenuated forms of matter which are said to be not even material—there may be some which act as vehicles for psychical interchange. If such psychic waves exist the discovery is wholly in favour of materialism. It would tend to rehabilitate those notions of spirit as the most rarefied forms of matter—an ultra gaseous condition of it—which Stoicism and the Christian Stoic postulated. The meaning of " God is Spirit " could not be understood till this insidious residue of materialism had been got rid of. It is a retrograde theory that we are asked to examine and perhaps accept. The moment we are asked to accept scientific evidence for spiritual truth, the alleged spiritual truth becomes for us neither spiritual nor true. It is degraded into an event in the phenomenal world and when so degraded it cannot be substantiated. Psychical research is trying to prove that eternal values are temporal facts, which they can never be.'[1]

We do not associate ourselves with this quotation in its entirety, particularly with the sneer with which it opens; but we are drawn to the force of its conclusions. In pressing for communication the whole argument of the spirit-presence seems to us weakened. Material elements at once creep in. We believe that in the whole of the phenomena detailed in *Raymond* and in kindred literature, the ' grain of wheat in the chaff is the sense of presence,' but the tilting table with its strange way of communicating, and the weird happenings induced by the aid of the other paraphernalia of spiritualism, are still a real difficulty.

We pray to Christ. We *know* that He is present. We feel Him at our side. We pour out our hearts to Him. We feel that He knows all about our life and circumstances, that He loves, that He sympathizes; His presence and all that we know of His life and death make their own appeal. In themselves they are part of the answer to our prayer. We rise strengthened, encouraged, helped, comforted. But supposing the table at which we knelt in prayer began suddenly to rock and gyrate; supposing we had to spell out its tappings; it would degrade unthinkably the whole practice of prayer.

Why should it be otherwise in the case of those who have passed beyond these voices? We feel their presence and that presence is a strength and comfort to us. The thoughts that link us to them we may put into words for we are still embodied spirits and

---

[1] *Outspoken Essays* (First Series), pp. 267 ff.

part of a material world. To expect a communication does seem to confess an impossible view of the unseen world.

A little girl known to the writer used to show every present she received to her sister who died some years before. She knew that her sister did not see it with physical eyes, and could not speak in human language, but to the faith of a little child that was no obstacle at all. Communion was far above all that. Another child and her father are continually conscious of the presence of 'mother.' Nothing is done without the thought as to whether 'mother' will approve or disapprove. But they never dream of descending to the level of speech or conversation, let alone the employment of a professional medium. The whole communion of spirit is immeasurably above that.

> Thus do we walk with her, and keep unbroken
> The bond which nature gives,
> Thinking that *our remembrance, though unspoken,*
> May reach her where she lives.'

Surely no spiritually-minded person can read one passage at least in the Communion Service without feeling the presence of silent unseen hosts : ' Therefore with Angels and Archangels, and with all the company of heaven, we laud and magnify thy glorious Name; evermore praising thee, and saying, Holy, holy, holy, Lord God of Hosts, heaven and earth are full of thy glory; Glory be to thee, O Lord most high.'

If one may draw an illustration from the football field, we are as the players in a team in the presence

---

' Longfellow. *Resignation.* Italics mine.

To Those Who Have Passed

of spectators. They may not applaud audibly, they cannot join in the game, but every one who has ever played football knows how the *presence* of spectators urges him to play the game for all he is worth. And indeed the tensest moments of all, the moments that make a player feel that he would die rather than fail, are the moments when a hush that can almost be felt subdues player and spectator alike to silence.

It is the same in the life of the stage. Compare the efforts of actors and actresses in the last dress rehearsal when the great auditorium is empty, with those same efforts on the first night. That silent listening multitude draws all the soul from the players. The inspiration is enormous.

So the silent hosts of those whom we call dead are all about us. They watch. Perhaps they pray. They urge us with all the power they have to play the game. For the desire of those hosts seeing ' with larger, other eyes than ours ' is the desire of God. Our conduct brings either pleasure or pain to them now, as it does to God. Moreover they desire the growth of character in earth-spirits for their own sake. Hourly, earth-spirits pass over to them, and bring either spiritual poverty or riches to their commonwealth.

The exact note we wish to strike is so perfectly sounded by a certain widow in a conversation transcribed by Miss Lily Dougall, that we quote it in full. ' It is a colloquy between a widow and a modern vicar. The latter having lost his only daughter at the same time as his son was killed in the war, had been plunged into depression, and had received great comfort from visiting a medium through whose lips he believed he had caught characteristic messages from his children. In paying a visit he spoke of this in confidence to the widow, saying at the same time how inadequate he had found the ordinary consolations of religion.

' " Well," said she, " when I was young I lost my husband. I was mad with grief. He was all the world to me, and I was a silly little thing without much religion and with almost no faith; and I had the children to bring up, and no one to help me. I just raged against God for taking my James from me. So when the parson came I raged at him for calling a God like that good. All he said was, ' I don't know whether your husband's death was God's will or not. It may have happened because of the sinful condition of the world; but of one thing I am quite sure, and that it is God's will to be your Comforter.' "

' " Yes," said the vicar, " we all say that, but comfort sometimes comes through indirect channels, and I think that in Spiritualism God may be guiding us to find such a channel. Did you find the comfort of which he spoke? "

' " I will tell you what happened if you care to know," said the widow, " I didn't believe I should get comfort his way. I was angry at heart, but I was honest. I asked the parson how God could comfort me, and he said that God could be all my husband had been, and more. I was so angry that I got into the way of defying God in my heart. A dozen times a day, when I wanted my husband, I would say to

To Those Who Have Passed

God, ' Now and here, this is what I need, and you can't give it to me.' Perhaps it would be advice I wanted; perhaps I wanted to show my husband how bonny the children were; perhaps I wanted to tell him of the clever things they said; or perhaps I was tired and wanted a hand to help. I thought this was a wicked habit of mine, telling God that He couldn't meet my needs. But after a while I came somehow to feel that God liked the honesty of it. Sometimes I seemed to think quite suddenly and unexpectedly of the Lord Christ looking at me with a twinkle in His eye "—she paused for a few moments. " It was just wonderful how, some way or other, after a few months, the world was all full of God for me. I was very young and foolish, and I am none too wise now, but I have known a secret since that time that I can't put into words. But what I was going to tell you when I began was something else. It was one day a year after my husband died, and I went out with God into the garden to get some flowers to put on his grave, and there, suddenly, I knew that my husband was there with me in the garden—just himself, only braver and stronger and more happy than I had ever known him."

' " Did you see anything? " asked the vicar.

' " Oh no. I thank God I have always kept my five wits about me. If the sort of form he had were the kind my eyes could see, of course I should see him all the time, and not occasionally standing about like a silly ghost."

' " Did you hear anything? " inquired the vicar.

After Death

' " No, I didn't.   How could I hear what I couldn't see? "

' " How did you know that he was there? " asked the vicar.

' " I don't know how I knew—but I knew; and times and times since I have known; and if you want any proof that what I tell you is true, I should say, Apply the old test—look for the fruits! Look at my children. Do you think the foolish undisciplined girl that I was, could have trained and taught them as they have been trained and taught? What I think is that whatever comfort you got through your medium, I got a better form of comfort, for I found God and my husband too." '[1]

We may thus draw great inspiration from the thought of those spirit presences.   But let us not press for communication.   The means used may quite possibly defeat their own ends.   If we are to know the nearness of the beloved dead, that presence, which is spiritual, will be most readily felt in our own quiet spiritual moments, when our spirit is at its fullest activity, leaning out of the windows of its prison of flesh.   Let a man prepare himself by devotional exercises, and, sitting quietly in his room, let him think of the beloved dead, and the sense of presence—which is the central truth of Spiritualism, and the central truth of the gospel of the communion of saints—will come to him.   Primitive instincts of superstitious fancy will not thus be aroused.   The dangers of hysteria will not be encountered.

[1] *Immortality*, pp. 365 ff.

To Those Who Have Passed

More and more as one thinks out the question one is drawn to the conclusion that it is extremely unlikely that the dead will be allowed definitely to speak to us. They would reveal too much. So Tennyson speaking of Lazarus says :

> Behold a man raised up by Christ!
> The rest remaineth unreveal'd;
> He told it not; or *something seal'd*
> *The lips of that Evangelist.*[1]

And tradition has it that Lazarus was a melancholy and morose man till the end of his days. He had seen too much. He had revelled in a fuller life, and then—because human faith was so weak—he had, according to the Johannine narrative, been dragged back to the prison of the flesh. Is not that the reason why Jesus wept, not in sympathy with the mourners so much as because He had to condemn a free spirit, glorying in all the freedom of another life, to live again the limited life of the flesh? The life after death is fair beyond the scope of human imagination. If it has taken all the uncountable years from the dawn of the human consciousness until the present day to make humanity what it is, then what an eloquent comment man's evolutionary story makes on the question of his ultimate destiny. To suggest that our life after death will stand in as great a contrast to our present life as the latter does to that of the cave man is to make a comparison which does not go nearly far enough. Our pain and sorrow, for instance, which bulk so largely in men's thoughts to-day, will bulk, in the perspective we have then, as less than the tears that

In Memoriam. Italics mine.

stained our cheek at seven years old; though our childish sorrow at the moment filled all our little world. 'It doth not yet appear what we shall be.' 'Things which eye saw not, and ear heard not, and which entered not into the heart of man, whatsover things God prepared for them that love Him.'[1] The physical brain is made for a physical body in a material world. If all the glories of that other world were to burst in upon us now, that brain would be so restless that it would lead men to suicide as a way of escape from this life; or, what is more likely, it would give way altogether, and men would be robbed of their sanity. The human brain in its present state of development would be unable to stand the strain of such a revelation.

But as the Christ-presence, with no inherent revelation of life beyond the grave, with no communication, a presence silent and unseen, sends us on our way strengthened because we have proved its reality; so we may know that our loved ones, so called dead, are near us, and they too shall succour and comfort our hearts. And how much superior to planchette and tilting table is this :—

> O blest communion, fellowship divine!
> We feebly struggle; they in glory shine!
> Yet all are one in Thee, for all are Thine.
>
> And when the strife is fierce, the warfare long,
> Steals on the air the distant triumph song,
> And hearts are brave again, and arms are strong.'

'Therefore let us also, seeing we are compassed about with so great a cloud of witnesses, lay aside

[1] 1 Cor. ii. 9.   [2] Bishop How.

To Those Who Have Passed

every weight, and the sin which doth so easily beset
us, and let us run with patience the race that is set
before us,[1] looking '—not to the paraphernalia of
Spiritualism, not even so much to our beloved dead
who are the witnesses, but to their Master and ours—
' looking unto Jesus, the author and perfecter of our
faith '; until we pass to rejoin them for ever and see
the King in His beauty, in the land from which there
is no return.

[1] Heb. xii. 1.

CHAPTER VII

The Present Value of the Gospel of the Life After Death

I

THERE are two attitudes commonly taken to the life after death. Taking the lower form first, there is the attitude which seeks to evade the challenge of this world by unduly stressing the importance of the next. An unjust sneer of other-worldliness has been drawn down upon the heads of Christian men and women who adopt this attitude. According to them this world is a howling wilderness. They sing with great enjoyment

> Earth is a desert drear,
> Heaven is my home.

It must be admitted, however, that such people often contrive to make themselves singularly comfortable in the ' howling wilderness,' and often, when the time to go ' home ' comes, they manifest no home-sickness, but seem almost reluctant to leave the ' desert drear.'

Yet this attitude is not to be despised in all who hold it. There are many to whom life has become so hard and unjust that the escape which death brings is a very great and real attraction. To many a tired wayfarer the last steps of the journey are illumined

The Present Value of the Gospel

by the light which streams out already from the gates of the City of Rest; to many a sufferer whose daily portion has been pain, and whose mind has been obsessed by the mystery of that pain, the thought of a life where physical pain cannot enter, makes death desirable indeed; to the bereaved and lonely the Angel of Death comes as a welcome friend, since he opens the door to a renewed and closer friendship and to the reality of reunion; to the embittered, death means the consolation of final adjustment and justice. To all such, death is the great reward of life. Many indeed can say with Paul, without any hypocrisy and without any shrinking from the challenge of this world's need, ' Life?—death?—which to choose I cannot discern. Oh, I am in a strait betwixt the two, for the yearning that I feel to sail away from earth, and to haven me with Messiah. Better, ay, far better were this.'[1]

Another attitude and generally a much healthier one is that which asks, ' Why worry about the next world? We have quite enough to engage our attention in this. We shall soon enough be there and know all about it.' That attitude in varying forms is very common and has been often almost unconsciously adopted by people who certainly do not need to be reminded that this world is a probation and a preparation for the next; people who in fact are often fully engaged in responding to the challenge of this world's need.

It must be admitted many men feel that, for the ordinary life of every day, there is little practical help to be derived from a detailed study of the conditions of the life after death. But some of us who have been

[1] Phil. i. 22, 23. A. S. Way. ' Letters of St. Paul and Hebrews.'

present when men have passed out into the last great adventure, and who have dimly guessed what was passing in their mind at the supreme moment, would have given much to have been able to impart our own faith concerning that next world to the traveller as he ' fears to launch away.' It is too late. One can only repeat the deathless words of the Master about the Father's home, and in a sense that is enough. But the dismay which is sometimes written on the features of those whose ' last heart-beats tap at the door of eternity ' would not have been so blank if the subject had been robbed of its terrors by earlier consideration and thought. Another word must be said. In the majority of cases the actual moment of passing, if a moment of consciousness, appears to be a moment for most men of calm and happiness. May not the angels of God already be whispering words of comfort? Indeed may not ' He that died in Holy Land ' be already stretching out to them ' the shining hand ' to lead them into light. But a few hours before the end some men appear to undergo little less than an agony of apprehension. It is only when one has seen men die that one realizes that for them and for their loved ones who watch and wonder, yet and for oneself, the question with which this book opened is one of no small importance—' What happens to men after death ? '

II

The Life of the Ages.—The true attitude to the subject can best be reached we believe, by a consideration of the nature and quality of this Life of the Ages.

The Present Value of the Gospel

Our sub-title purposely omits the words everlasting, eternal, and the like. That this Life of the Ages is endless is certain. But that this is one of its least important qualities is no less certain. Jesus called it the Life of the Ages. ' In this consists the Life of the Ages,' He said, ' in knowing Thee the only true God.'[1] The Life is not a matter of innumerable years. It is concerned with the exploration of God, leading to deeper knowledge and closer communion, rather than with endless æons. And it begins *now*, and unless recognized now will be hard to find hereafter.

In his *Natural Law in the Spiritual World*, Drummond has a very skilful analogy.[2] ' Life,' he says, ' is correspondence with environment.' As soon as correspondence with environment ceases, death occurs. As soon as the ear cannot correspond with the vibrations of the air, to all intents and purposes it is dead. The same is true of the eye and the vibrations in the ether. The greater the correspondence, the fuller the life, and vice versa. Eternal Life is thus conceived as perfect correspondence with a perfect environment.

' Uninterrupted correspondence with a perfect environment,' says Drummond, ' is eternal life according to Science. " This is life Eternal," said Christ, " that they may know Thee, the only true God and Jesus Christ whom Thou hast sent." Life eternal is to know God. To know God is to correspond with God. To correspond with God is to correspond with a Perfect Environment. And the organism which

[1] John xvii. 3 (Weymouth).
[2] *Natural Law in the Spiritual World*, p. 58.

After Death

attains to this, must, in the nature of things, live
for ever.' Man's spirit in constant touch with God is
immortal. Man thus shares the very life of God.
This Life of the Ages within himself *is* God manifesting His activity in man.

The note we desire to strike has been sounded
excellently in the poem of Percy Ainsworth's called
' And the Life Everlasting.'

It will not meet us where the shadows fall
  Beside the sea that bounds the Evening Land;
It will not greet us with its first clear call
  When Death has borne us to the further strand.

It is not something yet to be revealed—
  The everlasting life,—'tis here and now;
Passing unseen because our eyes are sealed
  With blindness for the pride upon our brow.

It dwells not in innumerable years;
  It is the breath of God in timeless things—
The strong, divine persistence that inheres
  In love's red pulses and in faith's white wings.

It is the power whereby low lives aspire
  Unto the doing of a selfless deed,
Unto the slaying of a soft desire,
  In service of a high, unworldly creed.

It is the treasure that is ours to hold
  Secure, while all things else are turned to dust;
That priceless and imperishable gold
  Beyond the scathe of robber and of rust.

And if we feel it not amid our strife,
  In all our toiling and in all our pain—
This rhythmic pulsing of eternal life—
  Then do we work and suffer here in vain.

The Present Value of the Gospel

In *The Cross in Christian Experience*,[1] Prof. W. M. Clow says that when the Kingsway, running between Holborn and the Strand, was being made, the ground was cleared of very old buildings, and it lay for a year exposed to the light and the air and the rain. ' A strange sight drew naturalists to the ruins. In some cases the soil had not felt the touch of spring since the day when the Romans sailed up the Thames and beached upon its strand. When the sunlight poured its life upon this uncovered soil a host of flowers sprang up. Some were unknown in England. They were plants which the Romans has brought with them. Hidden away in the darkness, lying dormant under the mass of bricks and mortar, they seemed to have died. But they were not dead. As soon as the barrier was removed they sprang into the fulness of their beauty.'

The seeds of the Life of the Ages are buried in every human life. They have been sown there by the hand of God. Wherever Jesus moved amongst men He saw beneath the soil of sin and selfishness and circumstance, beneath the accumulated rubbish, those seeds : and it was ever His endeavour to remove the rubbish that the everlasting flowers might grow and flourish. Wherever His followers go the same endeavour must be made. The Life of the Ages must be allowed to bloom on earth.

And the presence of those deathless seeds is the test of all things. Only the things of Christ can remain. Only those things whose life is the Life of the Ages can stand. Things which are not in posses-

[1] p. 175.

sion of that life will perish finally. They bear within themselves the seal of doom. They are like mould fungi that grow in dark and damp cellars. Bring them out into the blazing sunlight and they perish at once. But those things whose life is the Life of Ages will never die. They bear within themselves the seal of ultimate triumph. ' The Church knows that because Christ is risen all will yet be confronted with Him.'

Just as men could not kill Christ, they cannot kill the things of Christ; those things in which Christ still lives. They plot, they plan, they seem to succeed, but they are doomed to failure.

> Still as of old
> Man by himself is priced.
> For thirty pieces Judas sold
> Himself, not Christ.

Throughout all history influences have been abroad which seek to smother this life. But God's glorious purpose moves on. It simply is not in man's hands finally to break the threads of the Divine purpose.

For two hundred horrible years and more, persecution after persecution, with all the horrors the Roman imagination could invent, descended upon the infant Church. But it was deathless. It had within it the seeds of the life that is immortal.

Never was a truer word spoken than when Gamaliel pointed out to the Council that if the work of the Apostles was of man it would come to naught, as every other man-wrought thing has and will. But that if it were of God they would never overthrow it.[1]

[1] Acts v 39.

The Present Value of the Gospel

The track of humanity's progress is pathetic with the ruins of those things which seemed to live and which yet perished because they had not within them the only life which endures. Military power, wealth, literature, and art, have not been sufficient to make the history of Greece and Rome pleasant reading. But the story of a humble Carpenter has captivated the world and still holds it to-day. The history of a deformed tent maker is immortal. What is the difference? It is the Life of the Ages! For lack of it Rome and Greece are the memory of a dream. The individual, the society, the state that would win through must lay hold on the LIFE. Without that there can be only the dust of corruption and decay.

It was said of the men of the new armies, ' You can fight them, and sometimes win; you can imprison them, starve them, torture them; but you can never defeat them.' Through all effort ran a deathless, unconquerable spirit. It is true of the purposes of God. Church membership declines, crime waves sweep over many lands, the Christian outlook sometimes seems depressing in the extreme. But queitly, persistently, surely, come in the tides of the Life which cannot be stayed.

> Say not the struggle nought availeth,
>   The labour and the wounds are vain,
> The enemy faints not, nor faileth,
>   And as things have been they remain.
>
> For while the tired waves, vainly breaking,
>   Seem here no painful inch to gain,
> Far back, through creeks and inlets making,
>   Comes silent, flooding in, the main.'

[1] Arthur Hugh Clough.

After Death

Very widespread already is this wondrous life. It can be seen in lonely individual lives here and there. And here and there in great business houses; in movements towards real reform; in the ideals of nations; in the demand for reconstruction. Every changed life, every beautiful idea, every noble purpose, every slaying of the self, every bit of true progress in every imaginable sphere; these are the indications of that deep and real life, the Life of the Ages, being lived already here on earth. Here is the pulsing of the eternal through the temporal. Here are the buds of heaven bursting through among the thorns and thistles of earth.

At present we can only say ' Lo, here ! Lo, there ! ' but quietly, even silently, without the world's knowledge, without applause, almost secretly, as ' a thief in the night,' Christ is coming into His own. Humanity is as the body of the paralytic. Its effort is weak, its power feeble. But at the word of the Great Healer, new power—the Life of the Ages—is stealing through the clogged veins; stirring in the dead tissues; till finally the whole body, pulsing with that Life, shall arise in irresistible power; a new body—the Church, if you like—but the undivided body of Christ, inclusive at last of all humanity, will arise, and no citadel of evil shall remain. Now are only visible the signs of life, but as Jesus said, it shall be like the lightning which cometh forth from the east and is seen even unto the west.[1] In a flash it shall burst out, manifesting itself in world wide glory. Christ will have come in power.

[1] Cf. Matthew xxiv. 27.

The Present Value of the Gospel

III

Seen in this perspective the Gospel of the Life of the Ages is the most important issue in the world. And it is no side issue, no mere theological speculation, no concern of a dim and remote future alone. Indeed all other concerns are side issues compared with this supremely vital matter of the Life of the Ages. Through every activity of life, the only thing that matters is that we should allow the Life of the Ages to express itself, and that we should infect with it, the lives, which, from day to day, we touch. Here is the only final and ultimate reality, in which Truth, Beauty and Goodness meet; the quenchless Life of the Ages which is the unresisting activity of the Holy Spirit of God.

> That God, which ever lives and loves,
>   One God, one law, one element,
>   And one far-off divine event,
> To which the whole creation moves.[1]

[1] *In Memoriam.* Tennyson.

APPENDIX I

'The most incredible and yet the most convincing fact of history.'

APPENDIX I

The Resurrection of Jesus

THE first thing to emphasize is that Jesus in a unique way survived death, and proved to His disciples and others, beyond the possibility of any doubt, that He had conquered the grave and was still alive. The recovery of the disciples fro mthe gloom into which they had been plunged by the event of the Crucifixion, and the consequent history of the Church throughout all the succeeding generations, are sufficient evidence of this basal fact of Christianity. The fact of the survival of a full, distinct personality, the same personality once manifested in the flesh, abides, and will always abide, as the foundation stone of the Christian faith. Whatever is said, this must be said, and it is hoped that the subsequent discussion, so far from lessening the force of that statement (which to the writer is a statement of personal belief), will deepen and enrich it.

When this has been said, however, we must proceed to ask the question as to whether the physical body of Jesus ever rose from the grave, and the question involved in it, namely as to whether Christ manifested Himself after His death in a physical body.

These questions probably sound more heterodox than they really are. Does it make any difference to

Appendix I

our faith to-day to answer them negatively? Does it lessen all that Christ is to us in our daily life now, to learn a fact concerning His physical body two thousand years ago, even supposing that that fact be that certain material particles, which once formed part of His earthly body, remained on earth? To the writer such a question matters no more to faith than the question as to whether the particles of His clothing still remain in the Holy Land. He Himself is gloriously with us, as our daily experience, not a historic fact two thousand years ago, proves.

Again, as we have pointed out in the text no modern thinker supposes that the actual particles of his own physical body will rise from the grave, though he believes that he himself will live on. No conception of the spiritual world will admit that flesh and blood can enter into it.[1] Indeed those particles are so transitory that none of them remain as part of the human body for longer than eight years. Admittedly Christ's resurrection may be different from any experience we are likely to go through, but, if our thoughts concerning our own life after death admit of a purely spiritual existence, need we regard it as necessary and basal that the material body of Jesus should rise from the dead?

If we are to posit a physical resurrection of Jesus, then must we not say that a physical body was received into Heaven at the Ascension? And is not this a mere postponement of the problem?

If we are to posit a physical resurrection of Jesus would not the disciples have pressed their services on

[1] I. Cor. xv. 50.

the Master in the matter of food and shelter? If they
had not thought of His post-resurrection life as spiritual
would they have been content to think of Him wander-
ing about Jerusalem without food or shelter?

If we posit a physical resurrection of Jesus, how
is it that clothing comes to be left in the tomb, and
yet the appearances to Mary and to the disciples are
of a clothed figure?

But the most cogent reason of all for supposing
the resurrection appearances to be spiritual is as Bishop
Westcott has pointed out, ' that, if our Lord had returned to life as Lazarus had done, the fact that He
was alive upon the earth might have been established
by a physiological test; but what can physiology tell
us about any kind of life but our own? If this physiological test had shown that the post-resurrection life
of Jesus was really like our own—carried on, that is to
say, in a body provided with heart and lungs and other
organs, performing their functions as ours do—then
the Resurrection would tell us nothing whatever about
another life, or about a spiritual existence of a different
order from our own.'[1] ' There would have been no
pledge of a new human life; the chasm between the
seen and the unseen world would have remained un-
bridged.'[2]

We shall try now to face the difficulties which
immediately suggest themselves to our mind if we
lean to the conception of an entirely spiritual survival.

The first is that the idea of a spiritual survival
is inconsistent with that of an empty tomb. Sugges-

[1] Latham. *The Risen Master*, p. 68.
[2] Latham. *Op. cit.*, quoted from Westcott, *Revelation of the Risen Lord.*
Preface, p. xiii.

Appendix I

tions have been made of course, though they are all improbable. The oldest is the most unlikely—' His disciples came by night and stole Him away.'[1] Canon Streeter notes that the suggestion has been made that ' the Romans, fearing a possible disturbance, took advantage of the Sabbath quiet, to remove the body out of reach of the disciples.'[2]

But it is worth while to ask the question whether we are bound to a belief in an empty tomb at all. Our best evidence for, or against, would have been found in the close of St. Mark's Gospel, which is the oldest and historically the most reliable of the four. But in process of handling, as it was passed from reader to reader in the early Church, a piece of papyrus about twelve inches long, on which the end of the Gospel was written, got torn off and lost. We do not know what the last verses after verse 8 were, nor whether they were written by St. Mark at all.

In the other three Gospels, written at least twenty years later,[3] there is evidence of the empty tomb, and yet it is not evidence upon which we can strictly rely as historical, as the following quotation suggests, ' When the Synoptists undertook the task of composing their Gospels they laboured under this disadvantage, that the Apostles had dispersed in prosecution of their missions, and were inaccessible for inquiry and consultation. In the oral tradition they had, as far as it went, an amplitude of trustworthy material, *but it*

[1] Matt. xxviii. 13.   [2] Foundations, p. 134.

[3] Mark Circ. 50-70 A.D. Matt. Circ. 80-90 A.D. Luke Circ. 80 A.D. John Circ. 90-110 A.D. The earliest *documentary* evidence of Jesus appearing to the disciples is I. Cor. xv. 3-8, written about 55 A.D.

The Resurrection of Jesus

stopped short at the Crucifixion, and for the episode of the Resurrection they had to be content with such information as they could glean among the believers. This was all they had to work upon, and from the fact that their narratives comprise hardly anything beyond the visit to the sepulchre, it is a fair inference that they learned only what the women had divulged. And this meagre material would be distorted at once by the excitement of the moment (cf. Matt. xxviii. 8 with Mark xvi. 8), and by the subsequent process of transition from mouth to mouth. The result is, that in their account of the Resurrection, the Synoptic narratives, elsewhere so remarkably accordant, bristle with discrepancies which refuse to be harmonized even by the most violent expedients. It is hardly too much to affirm that, as they stand, they agree only in their unfaltering and triumphant proclamation that Jesus rose and appeared to His disciples.'[1]

We shall take the liberty of disagreeing largely with this quotation later, but it is relevant here to show that we are not in a realm of guaranteed historical accuracy. We cannot dogmatically affirm that the women, if they journeyed to the tomb, actually entered it. We do not know what they saw in the half-light of that early morning.[2] Mark says they saw ' a young man in a white robe '; Matthew says, ' An angel of the Lord descended '; Luke speaks of two men, John of two angels. A great fact emerges, a fact triumphant and sufficient. Jesus was alive. But from the evidence can we posit an empty tomb ?

[1] David Smith, *The Days of His Flesh*, Introduction, p. xl.
[2] Cf. Latham. *Op. cit.*, p. 53.

Appendix I

It has been claimed that the Romans would have instituted an official inquiry and search for the body of Jesus if the tomb had been found to be empty. But the fact that such methods do not seem to have been adopted does not seem strange if we try to think out the situation. Perhaps an Indian illustration is of value here. The position which Mr. Gandhi held during the Satyagraha Movement relative to British Official India, is not incomparable with the relation between Jesus and the Roman Authority. To the latter Jesus was the preacher of some new-fangled doctrines to the people. In their view He came too near the wheel of law and order, was caught in it and torn. After His execution His followers claimed that He rose from the dead. Those who first made the claim were not, for the most part, the educated or the cultured, but Jewish peasants. Officialdom hearing such a story, smiles, just as we laughed in India over the story related of Mr. Gandhi that, after telling some village women to spin and being told that they had no spinning wheels, he directed them to bury two strands of cotton from their saris and in the morning they would dig up a spinning wheel; or the story that on occasion he spirited a copy of the Koran through locked doors. So officialdom may have shrugged its shoulders. Dead carpenters do not rise from the dead. What funny stories ignorant people will believe to be sure! It is not an improbable attitude. If Mr. Gandhi died and some of his followers claimed that he had risen from the dead, who amongst us would even endeavour to prove or disprove. The story would be related at dinner tables in India as the lastest Gandhi-ism.

It is well to review possibilities but the conclusion which the present writer cannot avoid is that the tomb was empty. *The fact that the rumour arose* that His disciples had come and stolen the body is very powerful evidence of the empty tomb. And although it is possible to make out a case that a search was unlikely at the instance of Roman authority, would not hostile Jews have instituted a search, and if the body had been found . . . ? Certainly if the body of Jesus had been found and proved to be genuine the story of the disciples would have been discredited at once, and *discredited probably to themselves.* Even though to-day our faith in the living Christ may not depend on a bodily Resurrection, the disciples would hardly have been able to sustain faith in His victory over death, if they had found His body. Christianity would have died a sudden death, and no resurrection of that shattered faith would ever have been possible, unless Christ had been able to prove to His disciples that He had merely laid aside the body like a worn-out cloak and that He Himself lived.

Again it is difficult to accept the conclusion that if the tomb were not empty, then Christianity was built on the mistaken inference that it was. And though we may critically reject, as Dr. David Smith rather too sweepingly does, the stories of the post-Resurrection life of Jesus as unreliable, it is impossible to believe that they were purely legendary. In the apocryphal gospels we see the sort of thing that men's

Appendix I

minds invented about Jesus when there was no basis for them in fact. Dr. David Smith himself, in another of his books,[1] points to the crude pictures of a child-Christ who made clay sparrows to fly, and cursed with disease and death children who pushed against Him in the street. The post-Resurrection life of Jesus contains no such crudities. The stories must have had some foundation in fact. All four Gospels bear witness to the empty tomb. It forms the most reasonable foundation for the narratives.

The question then becomes this. Can we hold at one and the same time the theory of a spiritual Resurrection, and that of an empty tomb? If we believe that the post-Resurrection life of Jesus was purely spiritual, and also that the grave was empty, we are bound to go on to ask what happened to the earthly body.

The writer had come to the conclusion in his own mind that some kind of speedy dematerialization or evanescence may have taken place, when he was privileged to read Latham's *The Risen Master.* Latham's position is so skilfully and convincingly stated that a brief attempt will be made to reproduce it.

Latham imagines the body of Jesus lying in a stone recess excavated from the side of the cave or tomb which penetrated some seven or eight feet into the rock. His head is imagined as resting on a ledge of stone some six inches above the surface of the recess on which the body is lying. In front of the cave is a circular stone like a mill stone, running in

[1] *The Historic Jesus*, p. 37.

The Resurrection of Jesus

a groove about four inches deep. The stone can thus be pushed along the groove until it entirely covers and completely closes the low entrance to the tomb.

John reaches the doorway, finds the stone rolled away and ' seeth 'the linen cloths lying.'[1] ' They come under his eyes without his looking for them, he did not expect them to be there. The word used here is blepei (βλέπει·) Peter gazes on the clothes with a view to make out the meaning of what he saw (θεωρεῖ.) John . . . came in after Peter and beheld the sight and understood it (εἶδε.) John understood that the Lord had risen *because the grave clothes were undisturbed*, and on this evidence he believed.[2] John seems to have been the historian, as well as the eye-witness of the deserted grave clothes,[3] and his narrative suggests that when Jesus rose from the dead He withdrew from His grave clothes without disturbing their arrangement. On His retiring from them, the linen clothes fell flat on the rock, because their support was withdrawn, and because they were borne down by the hundred pounds weight of aloes and myrrh (John xix. 39). But there was no such weight pressing

---

[1] The word 'lying' suggests that the manner in which they were lying impressed him or he would have said that he saw ' the linen cloths.' Moreover the Greek word used (κείμενα) is as emphatic by reason of its position as it can be. He says βλέπει κείμενα τὰ ὀθόνια (xx. 5). ' That a strong stress is laid on κείμενα is shown by its being put first. If a Greek had wanted to express the idea of lying flat, or extended at length, this is the word he would have used.' (Latham, op cit., p. 42.) Peter also uses the word.

(θεωρεῖ τὰ ὀθόνια κείμενα, **xx. 6.**)

[2] John xx. 8. The Sinaitic MS. found and translated in 1894 by Mrs. Lewis has ' they saw and believed.'

[3] Though we cannot look for the same degree of historical accuracy or the *ipsissima verba* of Jesus in the Fourth Gospel as we find them in the Synoptics yet this narrative bears every mark of being autoptic, that is of being written by an eye-witness.

upon the napkin. Its smaller size, or the nature of
its material, or its three days wrapping, or all these
united together apparently enabled it to retain its
erect form, after the support which had moulded it was
withdrawn.'

Latham goes on to show that in the East, the
face, neck, and upper surface of the shoulders of the
corpse remain bare. There is considerable space
then between the garment covering the body and that
covering the head, a thought which, remembered in
conjunction with the conception of a stony ledge or
pillow on which the head rested seems to give point
to the words ' the napkin that was about His head not
lying with the linen cloths, but rolled up in a place by
itself.' The word 'rolled up' (ἐντετυλιγμένον) suggests
a turban or cloth rolled in turban fashion. An Indian
turban which the writer brought home months ago
still retains its folds, and would lie erect on its side.

The impression we get then, is that according to
some law as yet unknown amongst us, or to some
unknown combinations of known laws, the body
speedily evanesced. The clothes were not unwrapped
or the powdered myrrh and aloes would have made a
conspicuous heap on the floor. That no spices are
mentioned favours the view that they remained between
the wrappers of the grave clothes where they were
originally placed. If the body had risen or been raised
into an erect posture the spices would have fallen
down.

The witness of the grave clothes, which may be

The Resurrection of Jesus

thought of as a sign,[1] is certainly a valuable one. Had they not remained in the tomb, or had they been thrown together in a heap, the disciples would never have dreamed of a resurrection, but would have concluded that the grave had been robbed. A grave merely empty would have sent them home (cf. Luke xxiv. 12). Peter would have inquired of Joseph or Nicodemus. He would have been searching Jerusalem for His Master's body. Anxious inquiry and restless search would then have filled the hours which we know to have been filled with quiet waiting, a quiet, necessary after the shock of the Crucifixion, and as a preparation for the manifestations subsequently made to them.

They never seem to have supposed that human hands had borne the body away, and although one feels that there is probably a good deal of truth in the suggestion that the experience of the Transfiguration[2] when they ' saw ' and ' heard ' Moses and Elias, and became familiar with the idea of existence in a disembodied state, had prepared them for the Resurrection and post-Resurrection experiences, yet it was the position of the grave clothes which made true that simple declaration ' they saw and believed.' They seem to have realized that their Master had, by an evanescent metamorphosis, dimly comprehended as yet, assumed a purely spiritual existence.

Lest this supposition of evanescence or dematerialisation should seem a wild speculation, let me here

[1] Note in the Gospels the invitation to ' see the place where the Lord lay,' Matt. xxviii. 6; Mark xvi. 6; John xx 12. Perhaps this is the answer to the question as to why, if the body evanesced, the stone was rolled away. The open doorway beckoned to all Jerusalem— ' Come and see.'

[2] They were told to tell no man what things they had seen, save when the Son of Man should have risen again from the dead, Mark ix, 9.

Appendix I

quote some interesting sentences from Sir Oliver Lodge's *Science and Human Progress*. ' Will members of the human family on this planet, however high they rise hereafter in the scale, always leave a corpse behind them when they quit their earth life? Is there no other way of getting rid of once-animated matter? It is difficult to imagine the advances that may be made by the human race in, say, a million years : will this be one of them? Is there such a thing as dematerialization? There is evidence for it, though inconclusive as yet. . . . I cannot tell for certain, but it may be a true instinct which has led Christians to attach such importance to an empty tomb. It may foreshadow what ultimately will become a possibility for the race. If so, then in a new and real sense we shall recognize our Elder Brother as " the first fruits of them that slept." '

When all has been said obviously no explanation has been arrived at but merely another way of contemplating the mystery. That mystery remains. One almost feels that the central fact of Christianity must ever be in some sense a mystery, unprecedented and unique. ' We must make room for the possibility that the first Easter morning marks one of those great moments in the history of the world when a new power enters and begins to take effect. Like the first appearance of life in an inanimate world, or the first emergence of the conscious mind, it may have opened a new chapter in the unfolding purpose of God.'[1]

But another question suggests itself, and must be faced. Do not the post-Resurrection appearances sug-

[1] W. R. Maltby, *The Meaning of the Resurrection*, p. 4. The modern theory of emergent evolution does leave room for such a happening.

gest a physical, or at any rate a partly physical resurrection? If the post-Resurrection life of Jesus were purely spiritual, men ask, how did He manifest Himself to His disciples? It is impossible, perhaps, to answer the question dogmatically. It is not so hard to suggest possibilities. People have ' seen ' Jesus since those wondrous forty days. This was true in the case of St. Paul, and though vision and audition are in such cases supernormal, ' see ' and ' hear ' are the only words to use. Cases are known to the writer in which there has been no element of hysteria, but in which the presence of Christ has been so real, that those who have been privileged, speak not merely of ' a sense of the presence ' but of ' seeing ' and ' hearing.' And if we have authentic records, as we have, of visions of those whom we call the dead, appearing to those who mourn, with sometimes a definite message borne in on the consciousness by that experience, are we to say that our Lord may not manifest Himself in such a manner?[1]

The power to ' see,' that which is purely spiritual, and to have communion so real that the word ' hear ' has to be used, has been granted to many of our fellows.[2] Stories of such visions granted to the disciples, repeated year after year for some twenty years, might easily become the strange stories of the Gospel narrative of the Forty Days. Many of the post-crucifixion manifestations may well have been on the lines suggested by the author of *By An Unknown*

[1] Cf. Sir William Barrett, *Psychical Research*, p. 112ff. Visions are quoted on good evidence which have been seen by more than one person at the same time.

[2] Cf. The present writer's *Jesus and Ourselves*, p. 285.

Appendix I

Disciple in the last chapter of that admirable book, where a sorrow-stricken follower of Jesus, in the silent agony of bereavement, gradually becomes conscious of the Divine Presence by what may be called telepathy —though to give it a scientific name seems almost to lessen its value and sacredness. Is not this the way in which we to-day become conscious of the presence of the Risen Christ?[1]

Some of the incidents related of the forty days however, must not be treated too literally. The quotation already made from Dr. David Smith (page 151), though we think it rather too sweeping, contains, of course, a truth which we must frankly acknowledge. A story like that of the Way to Emmaus, perhaps one of the most beautiful in the whole Gospel narrative, and told with exquisite artistic taste, bears the marks of its own historicity within it. But some of the stories which would seem to bespeak most emphatically a *material* post-Resurrection life of Jesus cannot be so regarded.

The story of the partaking of food, for instance, occurs only in Luke (xxiv. 41-43). It is absent from John's parallel narrative (xx. 19-25). ' It belongs,' says a modern scholar, ' to the Synoptic cycle of unhistoric tradition, and is obviously a faint echo of John xxi. 5-9 and 13. It is remarkable that in Luke's narrative of the supper at Emmaus, and in John's narrative of the breakfast on the shore of the lake, it is plainly implied that, while He gave food to His disciples, Jesus Himself took none ' (Luke xxiv. 30, John xxi. 12-13).

[1] Cf. *Jesus and Ourselves*, chapter on ' The Presence of Jesus,' p. 243 ff.

The Resurrection of Jesus

On the subject of the touching of the body (Luke xxiv. 39) Dr. David Smith has an illuminating note. The passage is wanting in John's parallel narrative. ' Ignatius quotes the curious saying, though in a somewhat less gross form. " Grasp, handle me and see, I am not a bodiless dæmon," and Jerome says that Ignatius quoted it from the Apocryphal Gospel of the Hebrews. This reveals its nature. It is simply one of those unhistorical traditions which floated about the primitive Church, and Luke, ever watchful for new material, heard it, and incorporated it into his Gospel. St. Luke's story of the journey to Emmaus, and St. John's narrative (20-21) are the authentic and indubitable documents, and the rest of the Evangelical material (Matt. xxvii. 62-66; xxviii. 11-15, 16-20; Mark xvi. 1-8; Luke xxiii. 56-xxvi. 11 and 36-53), though valuable as testifying to the fact of the Resurrection is merely a report of common talk, bristling with contradictions. Here occur all the embarrassing crudities.'[1]

We have been trying to find an interpretation of the facts of the Resurrection which is in harmony with the laws of nature as far as we know them. And surely along these lines we shall be most likely to find a satisfactory solution of any problem. God is not to be regarded, we believe, as having made natural law what it is, and then, as on occasion working in a manner *contrary* to it. A view of miracle does not involve

[1] p. 44, Introduction, David Smith, *op. cit.* Note that a suggestion has been made that Acts x. 40-41 seems to infer that Peter represents the risen Christ as eating and drinking. ' It is probable that " after He rose from the dead " depends on verse 40, the intervening words being parenthetical. " Him God raised up the third day, and gave Him to be made manifest—not to all the people but to witnesses that were chosen before of God, even to us that did eat and drink with Him—after He rose from the dead." ' (*British Weekly*, Feb. 12, 1920.)

Appendix I

a belief in the contra-natural (that which is opposed to the laws of Nature), though it does involve a view of the supernatural (that which is above the normal working of natural law *as far as we know it to-day*).

Without acting in any contra-natural way, Jesus may have been using law that we do not know, or, to us, unknown applications of known law, or of course in some cases known applications of known laws, or faith without *knowledge* of law at all.

Again, we are beginning to learn a little about the power of mind over matter, and of spirit over both. When we consider what Jesus was in His mind and spirit, then none of His acts are to be regarded as necessarily on the same plane of action as our own, though this does not mean any denial of His perfect and complete humanity. With that perfectly pure spirit acting through matter and upon matter, dare we say what is likely and what is unlikely to happen? ' What if,' as Henry Drummond once said, ' it should be as perfectly normal for a sinless man to rise from the dead, as it is for a sinful man to remain in the grave? What if perfect nearness to the great Author and Sustainer of all should give a man power over all the tragic forces of Nature and time? '[1] The risen Christ had power to manifest His own purely spiritual presence through the senses of His disciples. Those senses were the only gateways through which Christ could pass in order to reveal His presence without frightening them out of their wits.

For the sake of clearness let us try to restate

[1] Prof. David Cairns. *The Reasonableness of the Christian Faith,* p. 153.

The Resurrection of Jesus

briefly the facts of the Resurrection in the light of our interpretation.

Jesus was ' crucified, dead and buried.' But His spirit, He Himself, could not be killed. Perhaps even that spirit was for a time numbed by the shock to the body[1]; perhaps it wandered in the world of spirits[2]; perhaps the three days' interval was a concession to popular belief[3]; perhaps it was foreseen that without that interval a strong case would have been made out that Jesus had not really died; perhaps the metamorphosis took time.

Be that as it may. On the first Easter Sunday morning a process of speedy and complete dematerialization or evanescence was concluded[4] and Jesus went forth to manifest Himself to His disciples and to others in a way which convinced them that He was alive.

Women came early to the tomb while it was yet dark, and thus the significance of the grave clothes was lost on them. They did not come to embalm the Lord's body, probably this had been done already by Joseph of Arimathea and Nicodemus in the sight of the women.[5] Moreover, their visit was thirty hours after His death, a fact which, in the east at that season

---

[1] It is interesting to note that Sir Oliver Lodge speaks of a shock to the spirit experienced after death by those whose death has been violent. *Raymond*, pp. 99 and 185, &c.

[2] cf. 1 Peter iii. 19.

[3] Matt. xxvii. 64; xx. 19; Mark ix. 31, x. 34; Luke ix. 22, xviii. 33.

[4] We cannot suggest more than that unless it be to point out that matter may be regarded as one manifestation of energy, and ether as another, and that there may have been a speedy process by which one expression of energy became another, involving the transformation of the former. Thus the same ego which was once expressed by means of the physical body of Christ, afterwards expressed itself through the ethereal body of Christ. The thought of such a change in the manifestation of energy is not beyond the survey of modern science.

[5] John xix. 39-40; Mark xv. 47; Luke xxiii. 55; Matt. xxvii. 61.

of the year, would have made embalming impossible.
' Their real errand was to see the sepulchre, if haply
the soul had reanimated its clay.'[1]

That longing in the hearts of the women produced
the psychic conditions most conducive to a manifestation of spiritual reality. And so He, who, on His
side, was also desirous of assuring them of His real
conquest of death was able to ' appear ' to them. If
He had appeared to them always as though His existence were wholly material the lesson of the Resurrection would not have been learned. If He had appeared
to them always as though His existence were entirely
ghostly, they would have been frightened, and then,
also, the lesson would not have been learnt. He
appears to them in a spiritual way with an appearance
of bodily form, since by that form alone could they,
in that hour, recognize Him.

' We may, if we will, believe that . . . the strength
of His spirit and love were such that He could give
clearer and stronger impressions of His presence than
other spirits can ; or we may, if we please, believe that
all the spirits in the next world clothe themselves in
some ethereal form, and that He had the power to
make this form manifest while faith was very weak.'[2]
At any rate, the spiritual presence became visible to
their enlightened eyes. Following this, Mary told the
disciples,[3] and infused in them the same desire to
prove to themselves that His conquest over death was
real, and at the same time produced in them conditions
most conducive to manifestation.

[1] David Smith, *op cit.*, p. 43, Intro.
[2] Lily Dougall, *The Undiscovered Country, Immortality*, p. 360.
[3] Mark xvi. 7; Matt. xxviii. 7; Luke xxiv. 10; John xx. 17.18.

The Resurrection of Jesus

So the fellowship of Jesus with those He loved on earth not only survived His death but was consummated after His death. Jesus carried it safely across the chasm of death and planted it in the unseen, ' making it the seed of a never-ceasing fellowship between Himself and men.' The same love which made it compulsory for Him not to leave His disciples without a manifestation of His continued life, led Him with characteristic restraint from appearing to those who had sought His death, knowing that He would win them only by fear, and a forced conviction was not within His purpose. And a like restraint is seen in that when He appears to Mary He does so as a stranger lest sudden joy should almost unhinge a mind already strained.

It is remarkable but very characteristic that again and again just as men recognized Him He eluded them (cf. Luke xxiv, 31; John xx, 17, &c.). It was as though He would teach them not to believe in His presence *only while they could see, or hear, or feel,* but to know that He was always there and always spiritually available. So He comes and goes, and they never know when He may break in on them, until they come to feel concerning Him that He is never far away, in fact that He is always present even though they cannot see Him. Gradually it would seem as if He schools them to the point at which they no longer need a manifestation. The aid of eye and ear becomes superfluous.

' He came " out of the Everywhere into the Here," that we might see Him and know Him, for our eyes

Appendix I

are not focussed to the Infinite. But when He had finished that which He came to do and had shown Himself so that we know Him it was expedient for us that He should go back out of the Here into the Everywhere, out of some men's sight that He might be near to all men's hearts.'[1] So He is with us 'all the days even unto the consummation of the age.'

[1] W. R. Maltby, *The Meaning of the Resurrection*, p. 18. (The reader will find a most beautiful and helpful interpretation of the Resurrection in this little manual.)

APPENDIX II

Surely He cometh, and a thousand voices
  Shout to the saints and to the deaf are dumb;
Surely He cometh, and the earth rejoices
  Glad in His coming who hath sworn 'I come.'
             Saint Paul. F. W. H. Myers.

APPENDIX II

New Testament Teaching Concerning the
Second Coming

THE earliest thought on the subject is found in the Epistle of St. Paul, and the greater part of it in the earliest of these Epistles.

In his first letter to the Thessalonians it is obvious that Paul believed that the Lord's return was imminent and he wrote accordingly.[1] The Thessalonians were somewhat alarmed. This teaching meant that those of their kindred and friends who had already died would miss the glories of the Second Advent. It was a strange notion, and it would be interesting to know what was at the back of Paul's mind when He wrote, ' we that are alive shall be caught up in the clouds to meet the Lord in the air.'[2]

As for themselves, the idea that the Lord would come again before their own death was the cause of an excitement and a restlessness which were far from being healthy. Members of the Christian community forsook their ordinary employment and became burdens in the little society for their maintenance and that of their relatives. What, indeed, was the good of pursu-

[1] I Thess. iv. 14-17 v. 2-3.   [2] I Thess. iv. 17.

169

Appendix II

ing one's ordinary work if such an Advent as they imagined were soon to be brought about ?[1]

In the second letter to the Thessalonians Paul very much modified his views,[2] and strove to quell the disorderly state of affairs.[3] ' The Lord direct your hearts into the patience of Christ,' he wrote. Gradually the idea of the Second Coming being within their own lifetime was given up, and later Paul's desire seems to have been, not to witness that great event but to depart and be with Christ; for it is very far better.[4]

Having regard then to the fact that the early Church, including St. Paul, were mistaken in their conceptions of Christ's return, we should do well to get back to the recorded words of Christ, which are as follows :

(1) ' Then shall they see the Son of man coming in clouds with great power and glory ' (Mark xiii, 26ff, cf Matt. xxiv. 29-31 and Luke xxi. 25-28). This has sometimes been regarded as a reference to the fall of Jerusalem which happened in 70 A.D., and which had just been descriptively prophesied by Jesus. Note v. 30. ' This generation shall not pass away, until all these things be accomplished. . . . But of that day or that hour knoweth no one, not even the angels in heaven, neither the Son, but the Father.' Whether the words may be so interpreted is not certain. It seems more likely that the words are a figurative way of saying that all the values for which Christ

[1] I Thess. iv. 9-12, v. 12-14.   [3] 2 Thess. iii. 6-15.
[2] 2 Thess. ii. 1-12.   [4] Phil. i. 23.

The Second Coming

stood will at last be vindicated. Love is the only real power and at last this will be made manifest.

(2) ' Ye shall not have gone through the cities of Israel, till the Son of man be come ' (Matt. x. 23). And yet when that work was completed no dramatic event occurred. But as the disciples gave their message, a far more wonderful and *effective* event was happening. Christ, through the words of His servants, was coming to human hearts. Secretly, that Kingdom of which He dreamed, and for which He died, was being built up. Did Jesus not mean, and did His disciples not understand Him to mean, that as they went about their work in the cities of Israel they were not merely speaking words? Christ Himself was beside and within them, seeking to come into the hearers' hearts. He was the power behind them and through them, and in every heart surrendered to Him the Son of Man came again.

> No ear may hear His coming,
>   But in this world of sin,
> Where meek hearts will receive Him, still
>   The dear Christ enters in.[1]

(3) ' For as the lightning cometh forth from the east, and is seen even unto the west; so shall be the coming of the Son of man ' (Matt. xxiv. 3-28 gives the whole passage which is the parallel to that already partly discussed in Mark xiii.). Secretly the Kingdom spreads in men's hearts. Here and there flashes of it are seen : in individual lives, noble deeds, lowly heroism, selfless acts, great movements, wide reforms; flashes only, but significant. Behind the clouds that

[1] Phillips Brooks.

Appendix II

obscure the progress of God's eternal purposes the power grows and gathers in strength. Sometimes a great part of the sky seems aflame, as when a movement of reform sweeps over a nation; or when the world is captivated by an ideal like that of the League of Nations. One day the fire shall burst forth—when the clouds are dispersed for ever—into one flaming response to Love Infinite and Omnipotent, and Christ will have come again to earth.

(4) ' Ye shall see the Son of man sitting at the right hand of power, and coming on the clouds of heaven ' (Matt. xxvi, 64; Mark xiv, 62). One day the position of Judge and judged will be reversed. The prisoner will be enthroned in power; as the King of the Ages He will judge every man's life. (See Section on Judgement.)

(5) ' For the Son of man shall come in the glory of his Father with his angels; and then shall he render unto every man according to his deeds. Verily I say unto you, there be some standing here, which shall in no wise taste of death, till they see the Son of man coming in his Kingdom ' (Matt. xvi. 27-28; Mark viii. 38-ix. 1; Luke ix. 26-27). The passage appears to fall into two parts : the first as some distinct manifestation at the end of the world; the second as though Jesus turns to the disciples in an aside and says, ' Don't be discouraged and think that it will be only at the end of the world that My power will be made manifest. There are some of you standing here which shall in no wise taste of death till you see the Kingdom of God come with power ' (or in Matthew, ' the Son of

The Second Coming

Man coming in His Kingdom '). And on the day of Pentecost they would remember His words. Here was the Son of Man in all the power of His Holy Spirit manifested in their midst. He had come back to them. They recognized Him. They could not see Him but they knew He was there. They felt just the same as they had felt, when, in the days of His flesh, His hand had been placed on their shoulder, and their hearts had been uplifted by His encouraging words, ' Be of good cheer.' One cannot avoid the conviction that those who had been His disciples recognized at Pentecost the spirit of Jesus amongst them once more. Had He not said to them, ' Lo, I am with you all the days ' ? And He had not failed them. There was a double fulfilment of His words. He had come back to them, His own loved disciples, in a special way. And He had come back in the power of His Kingdom to the world.

APPENDIX III

If the dull substance of my flesh were thought,
  Injurious distance should not stop my way;
For then despite of space I would be brought,
  From limits far remote, where thou dost stay.
Shakespeare (Sonnet 44).

APPENDIX III

Examples of Grain and Chaff in Spiritualism

Illustrated by communications recorded in Sir Oliver Lodge's book, *Raymond : or Life and Death.*

THIS book is chosen, with the special permission of Sir Oliver Lodge, because probably no work on Spiritualism has been so widely read during recent years. Though a work of four hundred closely-written pages, it has gone into fourteen editions in ten years. It is also chosen because in it the evidence has been very carefully taken down and sifted; scientific methods have, as far as possible, been employed to reduce to a minimum (what it is impossible wholly to eliminate) the possibility of fraud; and best of all, matter has not been omitted even though it has seemed ridiculous and absurd. One must pay an honest tribute to the courage which has refused to withhold that which might have, and indeed has, provoked the sneers and contemptuous laughter of critics.

We give first of all communications which are not out of harmony with Christian thought concerning the life after death.

Appendix III

1. (*a*) Reference is made by Raymond to the folly of living a selfish life, to the sacrifice of Jesus, to the method of triumph through suffering.[1]

(*b*) Reference is made to the growth of the spirit-body.[2] (Ether is supposed to be the substance of that body.[3])

(*c*) Raymond, speaking through a medium to his mother, says ' There's a lot in prayer, prayer keeps out evil things, . . . Raymond says keeps out devils.'[4]

(*d*) Hell is said to be remedial, not purposeless torture.[5]

(*e*) Christ is mentioned three times, and always in a way which harmonizes completely with what we know of Him. From our point of view in this book these are the most important communications of all, and we take the liberty of quoting them in full.

(1) (Sir Oliver Lodge is speaking. The answer came through the medium, Mrs. Kennedy, whose hand commenced the process known as automatic writing.) ' Before you go, Raymond, I want to ask a serious question. " Have you been let to see Christ? " '

' Father, I shall see Him presently. It is not time yet. I am not ready. But I know He lives and I know He comes here. All the sad ones see Him if no one else can help them. . . . I am not expecting to see Him yet, Father, I shall love to when it's time.'[6]

(2) The second is not recorded in full by Sir Oliver Lodge. Raymond tells them in a séance that he has

[1] Sir Oliver Lodge, *Raymond*, p. 178.
[2] Ibid, pp. 159, 187, 199.
[3] Ibid, p. 195.
[4] Ibid, p. 227; cf. p. 100, *New Revelation*.
[5] Ibid, p. 230.
[6] Sir Oliver Lodge, *Raymond*, p. 207.

been allowed to enter a higher sphere. He says : ' I feel exalted, purified, lifted up. I was kneeling. I couldn't stand up. I wanted to kneel. Mother, I thrilled from head to foot. He didn't come near me and I did not feel I wanted to go near Him. Didn't feel I ought. . . . I've asked if Christ will go and be seen by everybody; but was told " not quite in the same sense as you saw Him." I was told Christ was always in spirit on earth. People think He is a Spirit walking about in a particular place. Christ is everywhere, but not as a personality. There is a Christ and He lives on a higher plane, and that is the one I was permitted to see. . . . I am proud to do His work, no matter what it is.'[1]

(3) (Séance with Mrs. Leonard.) Sir Oliver Lodge is speaking. ' Have you ever seen that Person otherwise than at that time? ' ' No, I haven't seen Him except as I told you; He says, Father, He doesn't come and mingle freely here, there and everywhere. I mean not in that sense; but we are always conscious and we feel Him. We are conscious of His presence.'[2]

Side by side with that which has just been quoted, which may be regarded as helpful and beautiful, are communications which to say the least of it are extraordinarily puzzling.

(a) Raymond refers to houses made of stone and brick, having glass windows, without any suggestion that he is speaking figuratively.

(b) He refers to the reading of books just as books are read in this life, and makes many other references which convey the idea of a material existence.[3]

[1] Sir Oliver Lodge, *Raymond*, pp. 231-232.
[2] Ibid. p. 260.   [3] Ibid, p. 209.

Appendix III

(*c*) This reaches a climax when he speaks of smoking cigars and drinking whiskeys and sodas.[1]

(*d*) He speaks of such things as photographs and the like.

In the face of such examples, and indeed after a close study of the whole of *Raymond*, one is disappointed with the quality of the communications. Nor can we help being disappointed when a son—as is practically claimed by Sir Oliver Lodge—is in a position to describe for us the wonders of the life after death, and yet, in seven cases out of ten, sends a message to his bereaved parents, which is trivial even if it is not grotesque. Supposing even that the communications are genuine and reliable, a world is painted for us which all our instincts deny to be the final home of our spirits, and to which, if it could be proved to exist, we should certainly not want to go. No two pictures of the life after death could form a greater contrast than that of the spirit-world as Raymond pictures it, and the Father's Home painted by Jesus. And apart from the question as to which is the more authoritative, there is little doubt as to which is the more attractive and beautiful.

[1] Ibid, pp. 197-198.

Questionary

CHAPTER I

1. Is there such a thing as a *proof* of immortality, or even of survival?

2. Can an argument for our survival be built up on the basis of that of Christ?

   'For as in Adam all die, so also in Christ shall all be made alive.' What do you think St. Paul meant by that statement? Is it true?

3. 'To mourn for the dead, is, for the Christian, selfish, and thus sinful. It is an expression of self-pity only, for the one who is dead has gained immeasurably by the experience. It is like grieving because one whose companionship we desire for ourselves has been given a splendid appointment in a foreign land. As for the wearing of black, it is to succumb to a superstitious practice which in its origin is wholly heathen.' Examine this 'hard saying.' What is there in it of truth? What has been overlooked?

4. In leading Church music, why does an organist push in his stops when he sees the word 'dead,' or 'death'?

5. Dr. Denney once said, 'You cannot believe in Immortality unless you first believe in something which deserves to be immortal.' Discuss this statement.

CHAPTER II

1. What is the logical issue of the argument in par. 4 of this chapter, in the case of a man who for ever blinds his eyes to the heavenly vision? How does the New Testament meet that issue?

Questionary

2. ' Can the terrible handicap of a totally mis-spent earthly life be completely done away ? ' How would you answer the question ? (Consider the paragraph on forgiveness at the close of Chapter IV.) Is there such a thing as a ' totally mis-spent earthly life ' ?

3. What does soul-capacity for God mean ?
Consider the case of a child who passes over in infancy. There has been no development of a capacity for God. Will the next world, then, be entered upon in a state of spiritual bankruptcy ? Give reasons.

CHAPTER III

1. How would you comfort a father who had been brought up in the old school of theology, and who had been taught the doctrine of a physical resurrection, if the news were brought to him that his son had been blown to atoms by a H.E. shell, so that no trace of the body could be found ?

2. Interpret the quotation from Tennyson in footnote, p. 50.

3. What would you say to a mother whose baby died, and who asked you this question : ' Shall I know her as a little child, or will she have grown up ? '

4. Many thinkers have set their faces sternly against what has been called the theory of the ' Larger Hope,' or the ' Second Chance.' What is their main objection ? Is it cogent ? What is your position in relation to the theory ?

5. How would you interpret the following quotation from Tennyson's ' Vision of Sin ' ?

> ' At last I heard a voice upon the slope
> Cry to the summit, " Is there any hope ? "
> To which an answer peal'd from that high land,
> But in a tongue no man could understand ;
> And on the glimmering limit far withdrawn
> God made Himself an awful rose of dawn.'

Questionary

6. What would be the advantage gained by a final Great Assize? Are they advantages which you think Jesus would be likely to take?

7. Why hath ' He delivered all judgement unto the Son ' ? How?

CHAPTER IV

1.
> ' Come, Lord; come, Wisdom, Love, and Power;
> Open our ears to hear;
> Let us not miss the accepted hour;
> *Save, Lord, by love or fear.*'

Discuss the sentiment of the verse quoted (John Keble), especially the words italicised. Is there such a thing as salvation by fear?

2. Consider Charles Wesley's verse:

> ' Speak with that voice which wakes the dead,
> And bid the sleeper rise,
> And bid his guilty conscience dread
> The death that never dies! '

This sort of thing ' isn't done ' to-day. Why? What is to be urged in its defence, and what is the main objection to it?

3. Should we believe in an unending torment for the impenitent, even if all the words in the New Testament, including those reported of Jesus, could be shown to connote an unending duration of time?

4. Is the memory unending? If so, can there be any escape from an endless hell? Would Divine forgiveness after death take the sting from the memory of sin? Is reparation to those whom, in this life, we have wronged, possible from the other side? If not, is our own forgiveness possible even if we are penitent? If so, would this take the sting from the memory of sin?

Questionary

5. Can there be any real happiness in the next life until all men are redeemed?

6. What did John mean by the imagery in his Apocalypse? Collect instances and explain them.

7. How would you describe Heaven to a child of twelve?

8. 'It isn't fair that a man who repents of sin on his death-bed, should be forgiven.' Discuss this statement.

9. Do you repeat the phrase in the Apostles' Creed: 'He descended into Hell'? What does it mean? Has it any value?

CHAPTER V

1. What powers of the human personality will find scope in the consummated life? How?

2. Collect references in the Scriptures to the consummated life after death.

3. Can you dispel the 'vagueness of the poet' in the lines beginning

'Every evening at set of sun'?

What is 'the stealthy tide'?

4. Read Mark xiii. 32. What 'day'? Is the reference to the Second Coming or the end of the world, or both?

5. Study Appendix II. Could you substantiate the claim sometimes made that no prophecy of Christ's coming remains unfulfilled?

6. What are the objections to the older theory of a visible coming in the clouds?

7. If we reject Paul's authority to speak with certainty of the time and manner of the Second Coming in his letters to the Thessalonians, can we accept his authority to speak with certainty of the final victory of God? Give reasons.

Questionary

8. Collect instances from the New Testament which suggest the irretrievable doom of the impenitent. Set them side by side with those that are quoted in the text in support of the ultimate complete triumph of God in the case of all men. Can you reconcile them?

9. Are quotations from the poets admissible here? Give reasons.

10. Would one lost soul mean the failure of God's purposes? What is meant by saying that God is Omnipotent?

11. ' To sink back into that bottomless Cosmic " Mind-Pool " from which we were all drawn as water from a well ' (p. 104). Discuss this praseology. Does it represent the reality? Has man an immortal past? If so, is it personal or cosmic?

12. Consider Tennyson's lines:

' Sunset and evening star,
    And one clear call for *me*!
And may there be no moaning of the bar,
    When I put out to sea,
But such a tide as moving seems asleep,
    Too full for sound and foam,
When that which drew from out the boundless deep
    Turns again home.'

Notes especially for discussion the words italicized. Do the last two lines suggest absorption into the Divine, or Annihilation, or Personal Immortality?

13. ' When our Saviour declares that a sin against the Holy Ghost shall not be forgiven in the next life, He evidently leaves us to infer that there are some sins which will be pardoned in the life to come.' (Cardinal Gibbons, *The Faith of Our Fathers*, p. 213.) Examine the statement. Is it true?

14. Consider the hymn beginning ' Now the labourer's task is o'er ' (Meth. H.B., 836; Hymns A. and M. 401; Scottish Church Hymnary 325). Note verses 2, 3, 4, and 5. Do these verses imply universal restoration?

Questionary

CHAPTER VI

1. May a Christian indulge in Spiritualistic practices?

2. Have you any criticism to make of the word 'Spiritualism'?

3. If possible read Sir Oliver Lodge's *Raymond*. If not, study Appendix 3. What do you consider is the contribution which Sir Oliver Lodge has made (a) to Spiritualism, (b) to Religion, by his book?

4. 'Unembodied evil intelligences both exist and are at work.' Do you consider that this is a likely explanation of some phenomena? What does it involve theologically?

5. Collect instances of which you have heard or read in which 'spirits' have apparently been active, and ascertain whether there might be a telepathic interpretation which would as readily explain the facts.

6. In his recent book *Divine Service*, Dr. W. E. Orchard includes in the various services a number of prayers for the dead. But they are all enclosed in brackets. Why the brackets? Would it be a gain to introduce such prayer freely into our services? Would you hinder a child from praying to a loved one who had passed over?

7. Develop the idea that communion is better than communication. Why is it only with your best friends that you can sit for a long time in silence?

8. What does the passage in the Communion Service mean beginning 'Therefore with Angels and Archangels,' &c.?

9. Under what circumstances are we most likely to become conscious of the nearness of our dead? Why?

10. Discuss the incident of the conversation between the widow and the vicar, quoted from Miss Dougall. Do you think this is a common experience? Might it become one? How?

Questionary

CHAPTER VII

1. What is the danger of hymns like the one quoted :

    ' I'm but a stranger here,
    Heaven is my home ' ?

    Is there a similar danger from unduly stressing the other point of view ?

2. ' It dwells not in the innumerable years.' Why are the innumerable years unimportant in our thoughts of the life after death ? What value will time and space have in that life ?

3. ' Allow the Life of the Ages to express itself.' What does this mean ? Think out ways in which it could be done in the trades and professions represented in the group.

4. Read through the hymns by St. Bernard of Cluny (twelfth century) beginning ' Brief life is here our portion,' and ' Jerusalem the Golden.' Do they separately or together help us to form a true attitude to the subject of the life after death ?

Read the following three parables and elucidate the points they were invented to make clear.[1]

1. The pompous Mr. Jones died and went into the next world. Peter met him at the gate and said ' Good morning, Mr. Jones! we *are* honoured. Now what can I do for you ? What would you like best in the world ? ' Mr. Jones replied that he would like a fine house, with plenty to eat. Everything that could be wished for was given him as he asked for it. Peter left him for a thousand years. When he came back he said, ' Well, Mr. Jones, are you quite happy ? ' ' Quite, thank you ' was the answer, and Peter went away and did not return for another thousand years. Again he returned to find

---

[1] It is almost unnecessary to state that these well-known parables are not original. The author regrets that he cannot trace their source. They have all been repeated to him in conversations with friends, though their form has been modified.

Questionary

Mr. Jones quite contented. And again he went away for a thousand years. On his next return, however, Mr. Jones expressed himself as being the victim of ennui. ' By the way,' he added, ' where am I ? ' ' Oh,' said Peter, ' you are in Hell.' ' In Hell !' replied Mr. Jones. ' Why, I am a Churchwarden.' ' That doesn't alter the fact,' said Peter. ' If I am in Hell,' said Mr. Jones, ' where is that knave of a sexton, who used to dust the seats ? ' ' Oh, he is in Heaven,' said Peter. ' In Heaven !' said Mr. Jones. ' May I ask why ? ' ' The answer is simple,' said Peter. ' When he came we asked him the same question as we asked you, but his reply was this, " Give me the lowest place where I may worship God." ' And Peter took Mr. Jones to the top of a high tower and showed him Heaven, and left him gazing there for a thousand years. And when he came back again Mr. Jones said to him, ' There is a seat behind the sexton, maybe no one would mind if I slipped into it ? ' So he did.

2. A man dreamed one night that he was allowed to pass into the world of spirits. And when he got there, an angel came and said to him, ' Would you like to have a look round ? ' He answered that he would. And so together they went through all the courts of Heaven, and the things they saw were very wonderful and very beautiful. But the heart of the visitor was ill at ease for he thought to himself, ' This is all very fine, but how can they enjoy it while their brethren suffer in yonder torment ? ' And the angel read his very thoughts and said, ' Would you like to see the place they call Hell ? ' And, trembling, a little, the visitor said that he would. So it came to pass that they drew near to the gates of Hell. The flames crackled and roared and so great a heat was thrown out that the visitor thought ' We shall not get near enough to see anything.' And again the angel read his thoughts and said, ' But can you *hear* nothing ? ' And to his surprise the visitor heard strange and beautiful music coming from the heart of the fire. And he said to his angelic guide, ' Sir, tell me ; what wondrous songs are these which the souls in Hell itself are singing ? ' And

the angel whispered softly in his ear, ' They are the songs of the redeemed.'

3. A man who was entirely careless of spiritual things died and went to Hell. And he was much missed on earth by his old friends. His business manager went down to the gates of Hell to see if there were no chance of bringing him back. But though he pleaded for the gates to be opened the iron bars never yielded. His cricket captain went also and besought Satan to let him out just for the remainder of the season. But there was no response. His minister went also and argued, saying ' He was not altogether bad. Let him have another chance. Let him out just this once.' Many other friends of his went also and pleaded with Satan, saying, ' Let him out. Let him out. Let him out.' But when his mother came, she spake no word of his release. Quietly, and with a strange catch in her voice, she said to Satan, ' *Let me in.*' And immediately the great doors swung open upon their hinges. For love goes down through the gates of Hell and there redeems the damned.

Index

Abraham's bosom, 72

Adoration, 80, 92

Advent, Second, 93ff., Appendix II., 169ff.

Ainsworth, 138

Angel of Death, 135

Annihilation, 105ff.

Appeal, the Evangelical, 102
    to fear, 100ff.

Apocalypse, 80

Apocalyptic thought, 58ff., 94ff.

Atrophy, 40

Attitude to Gospel of Life after Death, 134ff.

Barrett, Sir W. F., 117

Baxter, Richard, 93

Beautific Vision, 92

Body, 24
    resurrection of, 47ff.
    spiritual, 49ff.

Brain, 24

Brooke, Rupert, 26

Brown, Prof. Wm., 114

Browning, 24, 67

Capacity for God, 38

Christ. See Jesus

Christianity and Spiritualism, 108ff.
    misrepresented, 90, 100

Clough, 141

Clow, 139

Coleridge, 73, 116

Communion of Saints, 118, 123
    with Christ, 43, 88

Conscience, 24, 40-41, 134

Consummation of Ages, 92ff.

Continuity, 20ff., 38ff.

Conversion, 45

Cowper, 100

Cross, 45, 74.

Dead, Communion with the, 108ff.
    interest of, in this life, 71, 73ff., 78ff.
    prayer for. See Prayer

Death, 28ff.
    fear of, 30, 136

Diabolical influence, 113

Dougall, Miss L., quoted, 73, 121ff., 127ff.

Doyle, Sir A. Conan, 108-110

Driver, S. R., quoted, footnote, 48

Drummond, 29, 137

Ego, 24ff.

Emerson, 22

Eternal fire, 59, 67-68
    Life, 69, 137ff.

Evangelical appeal, 100

Everlastingness, 68ff.

Evidences of Immortality, 20ff.

Evolution, 49

Final Restoration, 96ff.

Forgiveness, in relation to life after death, 83ff.

Friendship, spiritual meaning of, 44ff.

Index

God, inadequate views of, Introduction, 10

Growth, after death, 53ff.
  hindrances to, 39ff.
  principles of, 35ff.
  secret of, 43ff.

Hades, 72
Hadfield, Capt. J. A., 116.
Hankey, Donald, 32
Heathen, position of in life after death, 89ff.
Heaven, 38, 78ff.
Hell, 38, 67ff.
Henley, 34
Holmes, Oliver Wendell, quoted, 46
Hugo, 22
Hypnosis, 76

Idiots, in the life after death, 90
Infants, 55ff., 90
Inge, Dean, 124

James, Prof. Wm., 98
Jesus, attitude to immortality, 26, 27
  friendship of, 43
  His second coming, Appendix II, 169
  resurrection of, Appendix I, 147
Judgement, 58ff.

Kennedy, Studdert, 74ff.

Leckie, 58, 59, 99
Lodge, Sir Oliver, Appendix III., 177, 38ff., 48, 110, 113, 119
Longfellow, 20, 55ff., 100, 126
Lost souls, 102ff.

Mackintosh, quoted, 59, 102
Martineau, 22
Matter, 47, 163 footnote 4

McCabe, 112
Memory, 75ff., 91ff.
Mercier, 113
Micklem, 48
Milne, J. N., 30, 53
Milton, 72
Mind, the kingdom of the, 40ff.

Nature, of life after death, 47ff.
Newman, 41, 62
New Testament teaching, Introduction, 10

Omar Khayyam, 72
Optimism, false, 41ff.
Otherworldliness, 134
Oxenham, 33

Personality. See Ego.
  extinction of. See Annihilation.
  survival of, 23ff.
Physical life, comparison with spiritual life, 35
  curse of endless, 29
Physical resurrection, 48ff.
Porosis, 40ff.
Prayer, 118
  for the dead, 119ff.
  of the dead, 127
Predestination, 34
Preparation, 34ff.
Probation, 34ff.
Progress after death, 53ff.
Proofs of immortality, 20ff.
Punishment. See Hell.
Purgatory, 71ff., 89

Recognition, 51ff.
Remorse, 74ff.
Repentance, after death, 54ff.
  deathbed, 42, 86

Index

Restatement, need for, 8-9
Resurrection Body. *See* Spiritual
  Body.
  of Jesus. *See* Jesus.
  of the Body, 47ff.
Retribution, 63
Reunion, 51ff.
Roman persecution, 140

Sacrament, 43
Self, the human, 23ff.
Sheol, 72
Sin, effects of, 40, 76
  final defeat of, 101
  in the life after death, 56ff.
  memory of, 74
  vision of, 73
Slavery, 10
Smyth, J. Paterson, quoted, 24

Speculation, 9
Spiritual body, 48ff. *See also*
  Appendix I. on the Spiritual
  Body of our Lord.
  vision, 54
Spiritualism, Appendix III, 177ff.

Telepathy, 114ff.
Temptation, in the life after
  death, 56
Tennyson, 23, 49, 50, 52, 53, 68,
  83, 100, 131, 143
Thomas, Gilbert, 91ff.
Transfiguration, 108
Trevor Davies, 23

Unforgiveable sin, 104
Universalism, 96ff.

Whitman, 100
Whittier, 63, 100, 106